The Nor......
Or, the Robber's Raid ; A Thrilling
Narrative ; A history of the
remarkable attempt to rob the bank at
Northfield, Minnesota
The Cold-Blooded Murder of the Brave
Cashier and an Inoffensive Citizen.
The Slaying of Two of the Brigands. The
Wonderful Robber Hunt and Capture
Graphically Described. Biographies of the
Victims, the Captors & the Notorious
Younger and James Gang of Desperadoes

J. H. Hanson

Alpha Editions

This edition published in 2022

ISBN: 9789356906341

Design and Setting By

Alpha Editions

www.alphaedis.com

Email - info@alphaedis.com

Contents

—

LAYING OUT THE WORK

Between the 23rd of August and the 5th of September a company of strangers made their appearance at different localities in the State of Minnesota attracting attention by their peculiar bearing, remarkable physique, and decidedly southern phraseology. They would appear sometimes in pairs, and at other times there would be as many as four or five in company. At one time they would be cattle dealers from Texas, and again they were gentlemen in search of unimproved lands for speculative purposes, and then again they were a party of engineers and surveyors prospecting for a new railroad when they would make enquires about roads, swamps, lakes and timber lands, carefully consulting maps they had with them (published at 66 Lake Street, Chicago, 1876), and when opportunity offered Andreas' State Atlas of Minnesota. These men visited St. Paul, Minneapolis, St. Peter, Red Wing, St. James, Madelia, Garden City, Lake Crystal, Mankato, Janesville, Cordova, Millersburg, Waterville, and Northfield, putting up at the best hotels, spending their money freely, and creating a general impression of free handed liberality. But there was a certain air of audacity blended with their *sangfroid* and easy manners which led men to think they were no ordinary persons and aroused speculations as to their true character and vocation. The registers of the hotels honored by these guests bear the names of King, Ward, Huddleston, &c., generally written in one line, but subsequent developments prove these to be merely *nommes de guerre*.

On Saturday, Sept. 3rd and Sunday five of these strangers were in Mankato, and attracted universal attention by their peculiar carriage, suave manners, and fine, almost *distingue* appearance. They were well dressed and rode good horses, and sat their horses like men who were bred to the saddle. They made several purchases in the town, and one of them visited the City Bank and obtained change for a fifty dollar bill. When riding through the streets they showed their excellent horsemanship with a great amount of display and swagger entering into conversation with several citizens upon the merits of the animals they rode. They did not all stay at the same hotel, two of them registering at the well known and justly celebrated Clifton House while two others stopped at the Gates House, but it is not known where the fifth man put up. Two of the men, however, spent most of the night on the Sunday at a low brothel kept by the notorious character Jack O'Niel. This foul den of infamy is just outside the city limits on the opposite bank of the Minnesota river, and is surrounded by heavy timber. A more fitting place for a thieves' rendezvous, and for hatching plots or dark deeds, could hardly be imagined. It should be stated here, that after the visit of the two strangers, Jack O'Neil went to the Sheriff of Mankato and informed him that three young men—living in Mankato were plotting at his house to rob and probably murder an old man supposed to be possessed of considerable wealth, and residing at Vernon, some eighteen miles from Mankato. He made arrangements for the sheriff to overhear their conversation which resulted in the arrest of three young rowdies, Mark Ingals, George Peabody and James Quane, who were frequenters of O'Neil's infamous den.

A MURDER PLANNED

It appears that an old man named Gallager, living in a log cabin on the skirts of the woods surrounding Vernon, was supposed to have in his possession a considerable sum of money. The old gentleman lived alone, was known for his parsimony, and thought to be "a penurious niggard of his wealth." The plan of these young villians was to go to the house of the supposed miser, disguised, pretend to be "lost chicken hunters in the woods," and induce the old man to come out and show the way. Getting him into the woods they were to extort from him by threats the whereabouts of his supposed hidden treasure, if threats failed, they were to have recourse to torture, and that failing to murder!

O'Neil accompanied these scoundrels reaching the house of Gallagher about 2 o'clock. They enticed the old man out *a la programme*, one placing himself on each side of him the two others bringing up the rear. After getting some little distance from the house, and as they were passing a shed the one walking behind with O'Neil raised his fist armed with brass "knuckle dusters," and was about to deal the old man a stunning blow on the head, when he was seized by the Sheriff, who was lying in ambush within the shed. The three were conveyed to Mankato jail and locked up, and subsequently committed for trial upon the evidence of Jack O'Neil and the Sheriff. There are those who think the whale affair was a "put up job" by the notorious Jack to get rid of the three men who were in his way, *and this occurred an the morning of Tuesday, the 7th of September.*

JESSE JAMES RECOGNIZED

Returning to the five strange men in Mankato, they are next seen on the streets on Monday morning when a young man, Chas. Robinson who was acquainted with the notorious Jesse James, went up to one of them and remarked, "How do you do, Jesse, what brings you up this way." When the man addressed eyeing the speaker keenly from head to foot, replied, "I guess you have mistaken your man" and vaulting into the saddle, galloped away. With this incident, the five men who had attracted so much notice, excited so much admiration, and aroused many vague suspicions, disappeared from Mankato. The same day five similarly dressed, similarly mounted, and similarly appearing, strangers, arrived in Janesville, a village, on the Winona & St. Peter railroad, in Waseca county, about 18 miles from Mankato. As at Mankato they stopped at different hotels, two slaying at the Johnson house, and two at the Farmers' Home. No one know where the fifth slept, but on leaving the village on the Tuesday morning they halted some little distance out, and one, taking off his duster, rode back toward the village waving it over his head; he was followed in the maneuver by another when all four rode away. It is thought this was a signal for the fifth man, who, it is supposed, stopped at some house in the neighborhood.

Those, who stopped at the Johnson house, never made their appearance at the public table until all of the rest of the boarders had finished their meals, and during their stay in the town declined to admit a chambermaid to their room to arrange it. After their departure several packs of playing cards were found in their room torn up and thrown on the floor, and several handful of buttons of various sizes were scattered about, showing that the inmates had been indulging in a protracted game of "poker." The girls who waited on them at table, say they were quiet and polite, and never made any trouble.

Cordova is the next place these "gay cavaliers" turn up, all five of them staying at the same hotel, three occupying one room, and two another with a commercial traveler, W. W. Barlow, of Delavan, Wis., who describes them as polite, jocose fellows. They talked considerably of cattle, and from their language and peculiar dialect, Mr. Barlow thought them to be cattle dealers from the south. They left the hotel at 7 o'clock in the morning, politely raising their hats as they rode off. Cordova is about eighteen miles, almost directly north from Janesville.

The next night, Wednesday, saw these five men housed at Millersburg, about twenty-four miles west and north of Cordova, in Rice county. They left here at an early hour on Tuesday morning, and at about 10 o'clock appeared in the streets of Northfield, which lies about eleven miles north-west of the latter village.

On the same Wednesday evening, four men who answered the description of some of the bandits stopped at a hotel in Cannon City. The landlord thinks they were Bob Younger, Bill Chadwell, and the two men who finally escaped. He says that the next morning, the 7th, while three of the men were at breakfast, one retired to his room and remained a long time with the door locked. After all had departed, the chambermaid discovered a bloody shirt and a portion of a pair of drawers, one leg of the latter being torn off and carried away. The drawers were soiled with blood and matter, such as would come from an old inflamed gun wound, and it was evident that the wearer had such a wound on one of his legs. This is considered evidence that the man arrested in Missouri, in October, and supposed to have been one of the James brothers, was really him, but the alibi proved by that party appears to be sufficient to prove that it was not.

It will be seen by the foregoing that there were originally nine men engaged in the plot, which gives plausibility to the opinion held by many that the terrible tragedy which followed was the result of a plan conceived by some Minnesota desperadoes, who engaged these desperate southern cut-throats to assist in it.

NORTHFIELD

is a thriving, pretty, little village, situated pleasantly upon both banks of the Cannon river just thirty-nine miles from St. Paul, in Rice county, on the St. Paul and Milwaukee railroad. A neat iron bridge unites the northwest and the southeast sides of the town, and just above the bridge is one of the finest mill races in the State, the water in its incessant flow roaring like the ocean and appearing like a miniature Niagara. There is a large flouring mill on either side of the river belonging to Messrs. Ames & Co. The public buildings are not surpassed in the State for their beauty of design and adaptability of construction, and the Carlton college is another institution of which the town may well be proud. Placed as it is in the center of a rich farming district, the citizens are considered well-to-do, and the bank transacts a large business.

The five strangers appeared on the streets at an early hour of the morning of September 7th, and attracted a great deal of notice from the citizens, some of them recognizing two of the men as a party who visited the village about a week before, stopping at the Dampier House.

At about 11 o'clock two of these horsemen drew up at Jeft's restaurant on the northeast side of the river and asked for dinner. Jeft told them he had nothing ready, but could cook them some eggs and ham. The men told him to do so, ordering four eggs each. Their horses were left standing untied at the back of the premises. After ordering their dinner the two men went out into the street and after some time returned, when they were joined by three others and all sat down to their meal. They entered into familiar discourse with the proprietor of the house, and asked him what was the prospect of the forthcoming Presidential election. Jeft's reply was that he took no interest in politics, when one of the men offered to bet him $1,000 that the State would go Democratic. They still chatted on and seemed to be waiting for some one. At length they left and mounted their horses which were a sorrel, a cream color with silver tail and mane, a black, a bay, and a brown, all fine animals, sleek and clean limbed, and showing indications of blood. After leaving the restaurant, the five horsemen crossed over the bridge, two remaining in bridge square and the other three, riding up to Division street dismounted, and tied their horses to the posts at the side of the Scriver block. They then sauntered up toward bridge square, and after talking for some few moments leaning against a dry goods box in front of Lee & Hitchcock's store (Scriver block,) they walked back toward the bank which they entered. Three other horsemen then came upon the scene and commenced at once to ride up and down the street in dashing style, and calling upon the citizens who from their doors were watching the eccentric proceeding, to get back into their houses, commenced firing pistols in the air with immense rapidity.

Greater confusion could not be imagined than now ensued. Wherever persons were seen upon the street, a horseman would dash up to them in full speed, and pointing a long barrelled glittering pistol at their heads order them to "get in you G—d—s—of a b." The streets were cleared in a few moments and stores were closed in quicker time than it takes to tell it.

But though taken at a disadvantage, when many of the men were out at work or away chicken hunting, the scare of the Northfield boys was but momentary. Collecting their perturbed thoughts men rushed about in search of fire arms, but this most necessary desideratum for a successful encounter with a body of desperadoes or madmen, armed to the teeth, was found to be very scarce on

THIS EVENTFUL DAY

Mr. J. B. Hide, however, succeeded in getting a shot gun with which he blazed away at the marauding scoundrels, or escaped lunatics, for it was not at first exactly understood what the fellows were. Mr. Manning, armed with a breech loading rifle, came coolly upon the field of action, backed by Mr. L. Stacey and Mr. Phillips, while Dr. Wheeler armed himself with an old breech loading carbine and placing himself in a room (No. 8) in the third story of the Dampier House, delivered two very effective shots.

THE BATTLE

was now at its height, and firing was raging in downright earnest.

Manning, from the front of the Scriver block, Bates from the clothing store of Mr. Hanauer, and Wheeler from the window directly over the clothing store, and unobserved by the daring scoundrels, made it lively for the desperate gang, and kept them from passing into Mill Square.

One of the gang was about mounting his horse and while stooping over the pommel of his saddle with his back toward Wheeler, that gentleman took deliberate aim and fired.

The fellow pitched right over his horse falling on his head to the earth where he lay gasping for a few moments and soon was everlastingly still.

Manning in the meantime was not idle, and while Wheeler was searching for another cartridge, he advanced from his retreat and seeing a horseman riding towards him up Division street, he took a steady deliberate aim and fired. The man immediately turned his horse and started off a few paces rapidly, but the horse steadied his pace, the man rocked to and fro, and suddenly the horse stopped and the man fell over to the ground, when another horseman galloped up, sprang from his horse, turned the fallen man over and took from him his pistols and belt, then springing again to his saddle, he rode up the street.

Another scoundrel alighted from his horse and getting behind it commenced a rapid fire down the street, seeing which the intrepid and cool Manning, with all the *nonchalance* in the world, raised his unerring rifle and stretched the living barricade lifeless at the bandit's feet. The enraged brigand then ran towards Manning, fearless of the formidable weapon of Bates, and sheltering himself behind some packing cases under the open stairway of Scriver block, he commenced a rapid fusilade, evidently with the intention of keeping Manning from firing up the street at others of the gang.

But Wheeler had succeeded in finding another cartridge and returning to the room from which he delivered his first shot, a young lady, who had remained at the window coolly watching the fight throughout, pointed out to Wheeler the man who was keeping Manning from effectual work.

"Only aim as true as you did before" said

THE BRAVE GIRL

"and there will be one the less to fight" and Wheeler fired.

Instantly the villain dropped his hand upon his thigh, and the girl cried out, "Oh, you aimed too low," thinking the shot had taken effect in the middle third of the right thigh.

Wheeler at once left the room in search of another cartridge which unluckily he was unable to find. The wounded man who had changed his pistol to the left hand and discharged several shots at Manning, now turned about, and seeing Bates inside his store with a pistol in his hand and thinking it was from this source he had received his wound, as quick as a lightning flash sent a deadly missive at the unsuspecting Bates.

The ball crashed through the intervening glass of the store front, and burnt a scorching track across the victims face from ear to nose.

But during this time a bloody and terrible tragedy was being enacted in the bank.

A scene exhibiting a greater amount of reckless daring, and brutal ferocity; of intrepid courage, and heroic fortitude; ending in a most dastardly, and

APPALLING, SICKENING, TRAGEDY

could not be imagined than the one which was in progress in the bank while the street fight already described was going on.

Just a few moments before the raiders commenced their wild career on the streets, three men rushed into the bank, holding in their hands large pistols, the glittering barrels of which they directed toward the three gentlemen, Messrs. Heywood, Bunker and Wilcox, who occupied the desks behind the counter. Springing over the counter these desperadoes shouted out

"THROW UP YOUR HANDS,"

"we intend to rob the bank."

"Which is the Cashier?" one demanded, and instantly approaching Heywood, commanded him to open the safe. "I am not the cashier," was the reply.

The man then turned to Bunker, and made the same demand, but he also denied that he held that important post. The fellow next addressed the bewildered and fear-stricken Wilcox, whose terror prevented him from answering.

The baffled man again turned to Heywood, and with oaths and threats endeavored to make him open the safe.

Heywood replied that he could not, when the scoundrel fired a pistol close to his ear, and said "if he did not at once open the safe he would scatter his brains."

The brave Heywood still insisted upon his inability to comply.

The ruffian then seized him by the collar and dragging him toward the safe drew out a long, keen edged knife, and posing it over Heywood's throat, threatened to cut it from ear to ear if he did not at once open the safe.

But the brave man, faithful to his trust, stolidly refused, when the robber released his hold of his collar and went into the safe vault.

Now was the opportunity for the faithful Heywood.

"If I can but get that ponderous door closed," thought he, "and spring the bolts upon the scoundrel, the"

VILLIANS WILL BE BAFFLED,

"and my integrity saved from suspicion."

It was a supreme moment of dreadful anxiety to him, and such the intense excitement of his feelings, that when he rushed upon the door to close it, his strength was unequal to the task, and before he could recover himself to renew the effort, a powerful hand seized him by the throat, and threw him back from the vault, at the same time a ruthless arm struck him to the ground with the butt end of a pistol.

Taking advantage of this struggle between Heywood and the robbers, Bunker sprang to his feet and bounded toward the back entrance of the premises.

But before he reached the door a sharp report and the crashing of a ball showed him that he had only miraculously escaped from having his brains scattered by one of the bandits. Bounding out of the bank he ran madly down Water street, not however till another shot from the murderous revolver cranched through his shoulder.

At this point another of the band of ruffians hastily entered the bank and exclaimed:

"Clear boys, the game is up."

The three men instantly jumped upon the counter and made tracks for the door.

But one man paused in his headlong retreat, and seeing Heywood reaching for his desk, turned round and leveling his revolver at the devoted head of the faithful teller, fired, and without a groan, the brave man fell to the floor,

HIS LIFE BLOOD STAINING THE DESK

and seat with its crimson stream.

In the street the baffled and retreating murderers sought their horses and vaulting into their saddles they were soon rushing with frantic haste out of town westward.

It was some few moments before the citizens could sufficiently recover themselves to take in thoroughly the entire situation.

There lay in the open street a few paces from the bank entrance a bandit in all the hideous ghastliness of a bloody death. A few feet from him was stretched the lifeless body of a noble horse, while further down the street on the opposite side another grim corpse lay in a pool of seething gore.

Windows in all directions were shattered, and door posts showed scars of imbedded bullets.

Reluctantly the assembled citizens approached the bank, and the sight which there met their horror stricken gaze caused a thrill of indignation to seize upon every nerve; and strong men turned pale as they clinched their fists and set their teeth, registering an inward oath to wreak vengeance upon the miscreant perpetrators of the dastardly outrage.

There lay poor Heywood! the man who dared death and defied three of the most notorious scoundrels who ever "cracked a crib" or broke a scull, who resisted torture, and finally gave his life blood in defense of his trust.

Who was the man to carry the appalling news to the young wife and tell her that he, upon whom hung her very life, had left her for all time—that he had been torn from her and hurled into dread eternity by the ruthless hand of the bloody assassin!

Who was stout enough to bear the gore covered mangled corpse to the new desolate and grief stricken home!

But there were those who were willing to pursue the

RED HANDED MURDERERS

Some overcome with indignation, impetuously prepared for the chase, but others, perhaps more determined men, who were willing to follow on to the very death, were not so hasty in their departure, but as time proved were prepared to pertinaciously follow up the trial with the tenacity of the bloodhound.

Two of the former, Davis and Hayes, immediately sought for horses and none being so ready as those of the two dead robbers, seized them, sprang into the saddles, and were soon in hot pursuit.

Both men were well armed with rifles—one an eighteen shot Winchester with globe sight. At every point they heard of the retreating villians upon whom they were gaining rapidly. Dashing through Dundas, Hayes and Davis kept up the pursuit till at last they saw a group of horsemen surrounding a wagon from which they were apparently taking the horses. As the pursuers advanced one of the horsemen turned from the wagon, and advancing a few steps up the road ordered the pursuing men to halt.

Davis and Hayes instinctively obeyed, and strange to relate, these two men who had been so impatient to commence the pursuit, now that they were confronted by the audacious scoundrels found their courage waning, and they halted.

Nor did they again find their courage return, but they sat there and saw the marauders after securing one of the farmer's horses again boldly dash away.

After the robbers had gone, Davis and Hayes leisurely wended their way to Millersburg where they awaited the coming of the other pursuers, two men standing but little chance against six such desperadoes.

It is true that Davis and Hayes had the advantage of the bandits in arms, but it is doubtful after all, if there are many men to be found who would have done differently, confronted as they were by six stalwart fierce knights of the road well armed and unscrupulous in shedding human blood, as they had shown at Northfield.

After the departure of Davis and Hayes, about thirty citizens organized into a pursuing party, some mounted on horses, others were carried in wagons and buggies, and all set out in full speed along the road the robbers had taken.

Meantime the

TELEGRAPH WAS SET AT WORK,

and messages were sent to all points. Unfortunately the operator at Dundas was not in his office, and although the call was repeated for an hour no response was made. Had this gentleman been at his post, the people of Dundas would have been prepared to receive the bandits on their arrival.

It has been expressed as a wonder by many that the gang, before making the raid, did not cut the telegraph wires, but it appears from the confession of one of them, that their plan was a much better one. They intended to have destroyed the telegraph instruments before leaving, only the unexpectedly hot attack which was made upon them by the plucky boys of Northfield, completely demoralized them.

The first indication received at St. Paul of the daring raid, was from the following telegram to Mayor Maxfield:

"Eight armed men attacked the bank at two o'clock. Fight on street between robbers and citizens. Cashier killed and teller wounded. Send us arms and men to chase robbers."

JOHN T. AMES.

This telegram reached St. Paul at about 3 p. m. The first train leaving the city for the scene of hostilities at 4 p. m., was the Owatonna Accommodation, on the Milwaukee & St. Paul road. From St. Paul were dispatched, Chief of Police King, detective Brissette, officers Brosseau and Clark, and Deputy Sheriff Harrison. At Mendota Junction, the party was joined by Mr. Brackett and posse of police, consisting of Capt. Hoy, A. S. Munger, F. C. Shepherd, J. W. Hankinson and J. West, of Minneapolis, all well armed with seven shooters and rifles. At Rosemount, Farmington and Castle Rock, the excitement was immense, many persons at these points getting on the cars and proceeding to Northfield.

The train arrived at the scene of the most daring crime ever perpetrated in the State at 6:20, the whole platform being crowded with an excited populace.

THE DEAD BANDITS.

The police were at once led by the sheriff to an empty store where were lying the inanimate and ghastly forms of the two bandits who had been shot down by the intrepid Northfield citizens. One was found to be six feet four and a half inches in height; his body exhibited a splendid physical development, with arms and limbs of thewy muscles and skin as fair and soft as a lady's; his face was of rather an elongated oval with sharply cut features; high cheek bones, well arched brow and deep-set blue eyes. His hair was a very dark, reddish auburn, inclined to curl. He wore no hair on his face, but was closely shaved, and did not appear to be more than 23 or 25 years of age. He was clothed in a new suit of black clothes, worth about $25 or $30, a new colored shirt and good boots. The ball which brought him down entered about three inches, in a line with the left nipple and toward the center of the chest and completely riddling the man, passed out on the same side beneath the shoulder blade. On his person was found the card of the Nicollet House livery stable, St. Peter, on which is printed the distances of the principal cities in this part of the State. He had also on him an advertisement of Hall's safes cut from a local paper. His pockets were well filled with cartridges, and he had round his waist, beneath his coat, a cartridge belt. There has been some dispute as to the identity of the man, but it is now pretty well settled that he is Bill Chadwell *alias* Bill Styles.

IDENTIFICATION.

There were two men from Cannon Falls, who came to view the bodies before the interment, with the expectation of identifying one of the latter as a brother-in-law of one of the two. He said if it was his relative, a bullet scar would be found under the left arm. The scar was there, but the man would not say whether the fellow was his relation or not. The man whom the big fellow was thought to be, is

BILL STYLES.

BILL STYLES,

a former resident of Minneapolis, who has a brother-in-law still living there. This Styles left for Texas some time ago. It is said he was a desperately bad man. It is told that his sister received a letter from him a short time before, saying that now he had lucrative employment, and if she wanted money he would send her some. He also wrote in his letter that he would shortly be up this way, and would call on her. This sister was adopted by a minister residing at Cannon Falls. A letter recently received from the father of Styles proves beyond doubt the identity of the man. Styles' father now lives at Grand Forks, D. T., and says that his son has for some time lived in Texas. The father expresses no surprise at the untimely end of his son, and says he was always a wild wayward boy with whom he could do nothing.

CLELL MILLER.

CLELL MILLER.

The other man was five feet eight inches in height, but much stouter built than the taller, with hair of the exact color, and like his inclined to curl. His face was rounder and covered with about two weeks growth of beard; the eyes, like the other's were blue.

The clothing was quite new, even to the shirt, which appeared to have been put on that day. He also wore a white linen collar (new) and a white linen handkerchief round his neck. On his feet were striped half hose and good boots, but of different make, one boot being finer and lighter than the other.

Gold sleeve buttons, gold pin and gold or filled case watch and chain, with linen ulster duster and new felt hat of fine quality, "John Hancock" make, completed his costume.

Beneath his clothing he wore a money belt of leather, but it was empty. About a dollar and fifty cents had been taken from the two men, but Chief King, in researching this fellow, found four dollars more. The wound was an ugly, jagged bullet hole, very large, and with the edges much torn, toward the center of the chest and about four inches below the heart. There were also several small shot wounds on the body of this one and three on the forehead; his hat was also riddled with shot, and it was evident that he had been hit twice from a shot gun, for several of the shot wounds were in the back. From photographs sent to the St. Louis police, the man was at once recognized as Clell Miller.

SCENE OF THE BLOODY ENCOUNTER

The empty store in which the two corpses lay, is on Mill Square, which is immediately over on the south side of the handsome iron bridge which spans the Cannon river just below the mill race. On the north side of the square is the flouring mill of Ames & Co. On the west is Scriver's block and two or three small stores, among them that in which the bodies lay. On the east side is the office of the Rice County *Journal* and a wagon shop, and on the south is the Dampier House, under which are three stores, the last eastward and just opposite the corner of the Scriver block, is the clothing store of Mr. Hanauer. The Scriver block has also a frontage of 80 feet on Division street, 22 feet of which is occupied by the First National Bank of Northfield, in which one of the saddest and most daring tragedies was perpetrated—the heartless and deliberate murder of a faithful and brave man in the defense of the valuable property under his charge.

There are some four or five wooden buildings below the bank on Fourth street, and it was in this narrow space, from Mill Square to Fourth street, that the great fight which startled the whole country took place. Many indications of the fearful contest in bullet holes were found in every direction. Windows were pierced and shattered and balls must have been thrown around for a time as thick as hail, for the whole encounter took place within the short space of fifteen minutes. The conflict was a sharp and bloody one, and speaks volumes for the coolness and intrepidity of the citizens of the little provincial town.

From Mr. Bates, who took a prominent part in the encounter, the following was learned:

He said at about 11 o'clock his attention was called to four men who came from over the river. They came over the bridge and were mounted on four splendid horses. The men were well dressed, and Mr. Bates says, four nobler looking fellows he never saw; but there was a *reckless, bold swagger* about them that seemed to indicate that they would be rough and dangerous fellows to handle. Altogether he did not like the looks of them.

Again, at about 2 o'clock in the afternoon, as he was standing at the entrance of the store, talking to Mr. C. C. Waldo, commercial traveler from Council Bluffs, he saw the same men ride past—three came up the street from mill square and one down, street meeting within thirty feet of the bank. They dismounted and tied their horses to the hitching posts and two, he thought, went into the bank and two came down to the staircase leading up into the upper stories of Lee & Hitchcock's buildings, and here they stood leaning against the banisters talking. Commenting upon their fine physique, and upon their unusually good mounts, Mr. Bates and Mr. Waldo withdrew to the far end of the store to look over some sample trusses.

They had not long been so occupied when they heard several shots fired in rapid succession, and the thought flashed upon the mind of Bates at once, that the bank was in danger—Mr. Waldo stating that he cried out:

"Those men are going for the town, they mean to rob the bank." Mr. Bates, however, does not recollect saying anything, he became so excited. He remembers, though, rushing to the door, and seeing some men riding up from the bank—they came riding towards him with long pistols in their hands and called out, "Get in there you son of a b———."

Mr. Bates at once seized a shotgun and ran back to the door, but the gun would not go off. He then put down the gun and seized a fine seven shooter which was *not* loaded, and as the men came down again, (they were riding to and fro, evidently intent upon keeping people from going towards the bank), he standing behind the door jambs, called out.

"Now, I've got you." And pointed the empty pistol as if drawing a bead on them.

They turned their horses suddenly and fired at Mr. Bates, the ball crashing through the plate glass. There were other men at the bank firing down the street. The next he saw was Mr. J. S. Allen running down the street from the bank, and two shots were fired at him.

Mr. Manning, of Mill Square, whose store is adjoining the block in which the bank is, next came upon the scene. He ran out of his store with a breech loading repeating rifle, and took a deliberate aim and fired from the corner, Mr. Bates calling out:

"Jump back now, or they'll get you."

Next Mr. J. B. Hide came up with a double-barrelled shot gun and discharged the two barrels, and retired to re-load. Mr. Phillips also took a turn at the scoundrels, and L. Stacy delivered a cool, deliberate aim. Mr. Bates next heard a report over his head and saw one of the desperadoes fall from his horse. The horse made a faltering plunge forward and then suddenly stopped and the man pitched over with his face to the ground and in a few moments was dead. This shot was fired by Henry Wheeler from an old carbine from out one of the windows of the Dampier House.

Mr. Manning was still firing, and as he crept to the corner Mr. Waldo called out:

"Take good aim before you fire." Immediately after this shot one of the horses started up the street and the rider began to reel and swing to and fro and suddenly fell to the ground just opposite Eldridge's store. Another horseman immediately rode up, dismounted, and spoke to the prostrate man, who was stretched out at full length, supporting himself on his outstretched arms, when he rolled over on his back. Then the other man took from him his cartridge belt and two pistols, and, remounting his horse, rode off.

Another horseman, finding Mr. Manning's fire too hot, dismounted from his horse and got on the opposite side of it for protection, when an unerring ball from the breech loader brought the horse down, the man running behind some boxes which were piled beneath the stair-case before mentioned, and now ensued a

LIVELY FUSILADE

between this fellow and Manning, the scoundrel keeping himself well under cover, but a ball from Wheeler's musket struck the fellow in the leg, half way above the knee.

He at once changed his pistol to the left hand and grasped the wounded limb with the right, still trying to get at Manning. Finding himself getting weak, he turned and limped off up the street, but, seeing Bates with a pistol in his hand, he sent a ball whizzing toward that gentleman, grazing the side of his cheek and the bridge of his nose, and burying itself in a collar-box in the store.

Mr. Bates says he feels the ring of that ball in his ear still, and the ball, he says, he will ever keep as a souvenir of the hottest day Northfield ever saw.

The man limped away, and when he got opposite to Mr. Morris' store, he cried out to his retreating companions, "My God, boys, you are not going to leave—I am shot!"

One of the party, riding a sorrel horse with a light tail and mane, turned and took the wounded man up behind him.

MR. F. WILCOX'S STATEMENT.

Mr. Wilcox, the teller of the bank, stated that he, in company with Mr. Heywood and A. E. Bunker, were in the bank at about 2 o'clock, when three well dressed, powerful looking men entered by the door, which was open. They held large revolvers in their hands, and one of them cried out: "Throw up your hands, for we intend to rob the bank, and if you halloo, we will"

BLOW YOUR BRAINS OUT.

They then asked which was the cashier, to which Mr. Heywood replied, "He is not in." They then sprang over the counter and demanded the safe to be opened. Addressing each in turn they said: "You are the cashier," which each denied.

Seeing Heywood seated at the cashier's desk, one of the ruffians went up to him with his long, narrow-barrelled pistol and said:

"You are the cashier; now open the safe, you —— —— son of a ——." Mr. Heywood said:

"It is a time-lock and cannot be opened now." One of the men then went into the vault, the door being open. Heywood at once sprang forward and closed the door of the vault, shutting the robber in, when another of the men seized Heywood by the collar and dragged him away from the door and released the incarcerated robber.

The man who came out of the vault—a slim, dark complexioned man, with a black moustache, then called to the others to seize the silver which was lying loose (about $15) and put it in the sack. They did not do this, but seized about twelve dollars in scrip and put it into a two bushel flour sack which they had with them. The dark complexioned man, who appeared to be the leader, then again attacked Heywood, insisting upon his opening the safe, threatening to cut his throat, if he did not, and actually drawing a big knife across his throat.

The heroic and faithful teller, however, was not to be deterred from his duty, and would rather than betray his trust. Some few moments—it seemed ages to the bewildered and terror-stricken lookers-on—were spent in Heywood's struggling to break from the murderous villain and gain his liberty.

At length he broke away, and regaining his feet, ran toward the door crying

"MURDER!"

The man at once struck him with a pistol and knocked him down, and, dragging him to the safe door, commanded him to open it. But the intrepid clerk stolidly refused, when the villain shot at him, but did not hit him.

Evidently the shot was intended rather to intimidate him than injure, but the scoundrel had reckoned without his host, for the effect was lost upon Heywood.

But upon the discharge of the pistol Bunker made a start for the back door and ran for dear life, one of the robbers pursuing and firing, the shot taking effect in the shoulder. Bunker, however, reached the street (Water street) and ran to Dr. Coombs' office.

During the whole of this time four or five men were riding up and down the street, shooting in every direction, and keeping up an incessant fusilade.

One of the men outside came riding up furiously and called for the men to leave the bank.

"THE GAME'S UP."

he said, "and we are beaten."

The three men in the bank then sprang over the counter and rushed to the door, and Heywood staggered to the chair, but, as the last one was getting over the counter, with one hand on the cashier's desk, he turned round and deliberately fired. Heywood fell senseless to the floor! The man then sprang on the rail and out at the front door, and he (Wilcox) cleared out of the back door into Manning's hardware store.

Wilcox was not sure whether the ruffian struck Heywood when the latter staggered to the cashier's chair, and he did not stop to see if he was dead when he fell. He said the reason he did not try to get out or help Heywood was that one of the men stood over him with a pistol in his hand.

Mr. Allen said he saw three men cross the bridge and go toward the bank. They were all big, powerful men, well dressed. One had sandy side-whiskers, shaved chin and blue eyes. Another, wore a black mustache, and was a slight but tall man, and better dressed than the others. The third man was heavy set, with curly brown hair, and beard of about one week's growth. They had tied their horses and talked a while, when another came up, and he went into the bank. Mr. Allen then waited half a minute, and then walked up to the bank to see what was up.

"As I got to the back door," he says, "one man came out and grabbed me by the collar, and said 'you son of a——, don't holler,' drawing a revolver. I got out and made tracks as fast as I could, two shots feeing fired after me."

Mr. Ben Henry says that he was first attracted to the strangers by seeing the horses tied, and he went up to one and was examining the saddle, when one of the men came up and said,

"What are you doing here?"

"Looking at this saddle," was the reply "I want an article like that, and thought perhaps I could strike a bargain with the owner."

Drawing a pistol, the fellow cried out:

"Now you git'" And he *did* "git," but as he walked away a bullet came hissing by his head and struck a wall close by. Henry deliberately picked up the ball and put it in his pocket, but made long strides for home.

It appeared that the object of the men on the street was at first only to keep people back from the bank, and not a desire to murder indiscriminately, but when they found that the Northfield people would not scare worth a cent, and that real work was before them, they showed all the

SAVAGE BLOODTHIRSTY PROPENSITY

of their nature, and wherever a face showed itself, whether it was man, woman or child, the robbers fired murderously at it, crashing in windows in a lively style.

Early Friday morning it was reported in Northfield that Brissette and Hoy had joined their forces at Morristown and had a hot encounter with the gang, which had been reinforced by three others. The police succeeded in killing one man and capturing the wounded man carried from Northfield. The robbers then took to the woods and the police held them there. This report was proved at a later date to be a complete fabrication, but so excited were the people that every rumor received credence and grew in dimensions as it was handed round by the busy throng of news seekers.

THE BANK,

It is in a small apartment, about 20 by 50 feet, situate in the Scriver block, folding doors in the center of the front opening into Division street. It has a counter three feet high, running across to within three feet of the west wall, and going back the whole length of the building. This counter is mounted by a thirty inch glazed rail, leaving a space of two feet in front, where the men jumped over, scratching the counter with their boots. Inside of the center is the safe vault fitted with the Detroit Safe Company's doors, and to the left is the cashier's chair where poor Heywood fell a victim to the assassin's hand. A blotting pad lay upon the desk stained with the life-blood of the murdered man.

HEYWOOD'S DEATH WOUND.

Poor Heywood was shot through the head, the ball entering at the right temple and passing downward and inward, scattering his brains all about, and doubtless depriving him instantaneously of consciousness, and putting him completely beyond all suffering, although he breathed for about twenty minutes, but did not speak. In addition to the bullet wound, there was a slight scratch in the right side of the neck as from a knife.

BREAKING THE NEWS TO MRS. HEYWOOD.

Mr. E. E. Bunker was not considered dangerously wounded, the ball passing in at the back of the right shoulder, below the point of the shoulder, passing downward and forward and upward, coming out just above the clavicle, making only a severe flesh wound. This wound, however, was very nearly being a fatal one, as the ball passed close to a principal artery, which no doubt, had it been severed by the deadly missive, would have produced death by hemorrhage.

Since the capture at Madelia of the Younger boys, Mr. Bunker has given his recollections of the bank raid, and as it differs in several points from others already given, we embody it in this narrative. It will be seen that the narrative recognizes two of the men who entered the bank as Charley.Pitts and Bob Younger.

MR. E. E. BUNKER'S STORY.

Mr. Bunker said that himself, Mr. Heywood and Mr. Wilcox were sitting at their respective desks, when they heard a heavy rush from the bank door to the counter. They turned round and saw three men climbing over the counter and with their knees on it and revolvers pointed directly at the three bank officers. A man presumed to be Jesse James, and who acted as leader, called out, "Throw up your hands, we are going to rob the bank." James then ran across the room and passed Heywood into the vault, which was open, but seeing the safe door closed, turned back from the entrance and seizing Heywood by the collar who, from being older than the others and from the position of his desk, was naturally supposed to be the cashier, ordered him to open the safe, Mr. Heywood said it was a time lock, and it could not be opened. The other said that was a d—d lie.

Charley Pitts then came up on the other side of Heywood and threatened to kill him if he did not immediately open the safe. One of the others called out, "Let's cut his throat and be done with it." Heywood commenced shouting murder and repeated the cry three or four times. They then hustled him about, and James struck him on the head with the butt end of his pistol, knocking him down. He was then dragged towards the vault, where he lay with his head partially in the vault. James then drew the knife across Heywood's neck, who did not say anything, appearing to be partially insensible, when another of them stooped down and fired close to the prostrate man's head, the ball penetrating a tin box containing papers in the vault.

All this time I was on my knees on the floor, with Bob Younger standing guard over me. I had a revolver under the counter, where I stand, and which was in full view, and I endeavored gradually to edge over and obtain possession of it, but Bob saw the attempt, and seeing the weapon, put it into his pocket, saying, at the same time, that I could do nothing with this, and it was of no use. He then placed it in his pocket and commenced searching me, but did not take anything from me. The pistol was a Smith & Wesson, and we always regarded it as an excellent weapon. Bob having turned his head partially around to see what was going on in the other part of the room, I raised my head with the view of giving the alarm to any one I saw in the street, but my movements were quickly observed by Bob who pulled me down, saying at the same time, that I had better keep quiet for, if I attempted to rise again he would kill me. He then inquired where was the cashier's till, and I pointed to a box containing some nickels and scrip, the former done up in cartridges. He seemed to know very well there was more loose money than that, and he told me he would kill me if I did not show him the till. I did not answer him, and he pulled out a drawer containing stationery, but the drawer having some $2,000 he did not open, supposing, probably, that in its contents were the same.

Meantime, while the two men were engaged with Heywood, James told Bob Younger to bring out the sack. Bob took out a green bag and thrust a handful of scrip into it, but did not take any of the nickels.

The distance from where I was to the rear of the bank, is about 25 feet, and the rear door of the two hardware stores adjoin the rear door of the bank. I thought if I could make my way out in this direction, I would have a chance of giving the alarm, so that the citizens would come to the rescue. In making this movement, I should have to pass where Mr. Wilcox was sitting, and I made a slight motion for him to move so that I could get past. He saw my motion and shifted his position. The man who stood over me having his attention directed to the proceedings of the others, I started, but was immediately followed by Charley Pitts, who fired at me, the ball going through the blinds of the door and lodging in a brick chimney, but not striking me. There was a stairway leading down, and Pitts standing on top of that, fired down on me, I having reached the bottom at the time, fired again, the ball just striking me below the scapula, passing through the thin portion of it, and down, passing out about half an inch below the collar bone, the course traversed being about seven inches, and narrowly missing the sub-claviel artery, where the wound would have been fatal.

I think it was James that said, while keeping us down, "don't one of you move; we have fifty men on the street, and you will be killed if you move." The safe was not locked at all, but there was only about $15,000 in it, which they might easily have secured.

Mr. Bunker said he recognized the body killed at Madelia, as that of Charley Pitts, and also identified Bob Younger, by the likeness published herein.

NICHOLAS GUSTAVSON.

Several citizens of Northfield narrowly escaped with their lives during the encounter. A Norwegian, Nicholas Gustavson by name, was struck with a bullet at the right side of the head, just at the ear, the ball running under the scalp and out at the top of his head. He says when he was struck, and for several minutes after, his whole left side was paralyzed. But after a few minutes of unconsciousness, he was able to reach his boarding house, but the next day he was unable to rise from his bed. It was evident that the skull was fractured, and depressing upon the right lobe of the brain, and if the patient was not opportunely relieved by trepanning the skull, the man must succumb. Subsequent events proved the correctness of this view, for the operation was not performed, and the poor fellow expired on the eleventh—four days after the dreadful tragedy, thus adding another victim to rekindle the fire of indignation in men's minds.

Illustrative of the dangerous nature of the weapons of the lawless ruffians carried, it should have been stated that balls fired from one side of Mill Square struck and completely riddled buildings on the other side of the square, a distance of one hundred and fifty yards.

THE INQUEST.

Friday afternoon the coroner, Dr. Waugh, from Faribault, held an inquest upon the bodies of the two scoundrels who met with such a richly deserved end, and the following gentlemen were sworn as a jury: A. H. Rawson, S. L. Bushnell, R. Silk, J. L. McFee, R. Plummer and C. W. Gross. The jury were not long in arriving at the following verdict: "That the two unknown men came to their deaths by the discharge of firearms in the hands of our citizens in self-defense and in protecting the property of the First National Bank of Northfield."

The same jury, with the coroner, held an inquest over the remains of the lamented victim of the raid. The witnesses who gave evidence were E. Hobbs, ex policeman J. S. Allen, F. Wilcox and E. L. Fuller, whose statements were similar to those the same gentlemen made to the writer, and recorded elsewhere in these pages. The verdict found was: "That J. H. Heywood came to his death by a pistol shot fired by an unknown man attempting to rob the First National Bank of Northfield."

THE ROBBER HUNT.

ON THE ROAD.

The desperate freebooters had dashed from Northfield with but five horses, one, the brown mare carrying double. They rushed ruthlessly on, taking the entire road, and demanding that those they met should "take to the ditch." A short distance out of the city an old German farmer with his heavy team loaded with "garden truck," met them on a narrow road on each side of which were deep gullies. Drawing his pistol the leader exclaimed with an oath, "take the ditch G——d d——n you." Over the old fellow went scattering his vegetables, breaking his wagon and harness, and sprawling himself in a sea of stagnant mire.

After several hours the frightened agriculturist succeeded in getting to town, and related a wonderful story of being attacked by fifty giants fifteen feet high, mounted on fire breathing steeds, and carrying twenty-five pound cannons in their hands!

THE DASH THROUGH DUNDAS

was made at full speed, causing the greatest excitement. All were now mounted, but a horse taken from a farrier, Empey, near Northfield, evidently found it difficult to keep pace with the trained nags belonging to the robbers.

A short distance out of Dundas the gang stopped at a farm house and borrowed a pail which they took to a spring near by. Here they paused long enough to water their animals, and wash the desperate wound which Bob Younger, (as was afterwards found) had received directly through his right elbow, and which besides bleeding profusely had become almost unbearable, even to a man of his determination and vigor. Throwing the pail by the side of the road, the squad hastened on, little thinking of the pursuit which was being organized in the rear.

As it is now known that the squad, as it now remained, consisted of Cole, Jim and Bob Younger, Charlie Pitts, and probably the James boys, their names will be used in this narrative hereafter, wherever they are known from their own statements to have been.

As the horse taken from the farmer Empey of course wore no saddle, it became necessary for the comfort of its rider that one be impressed. To accomplish this, two of the gang called at the house of a farmer living a short distance from the road, and telling that

THEY WERE OFFICERS AFTER HORSE THIEVES,

borrowed a saddle. This took place at 4½ o'clock, and a half hour before, the landlord of Cushman's Hotel in Millersburg saw the other four pass his house on a gallop. He says that three of them stopped at his hostelry the night before. He saw the other two pass some time later, but did not recognize among the six, the man that made up four whom he had entertained.

Mr. Cushman says the men were extremely well-behaved, using no liquor, and indulging in no profanity or vulgarity. They retired early and arose late. He speaks of one as evidently the leader, he appearing like a man who had never done any manual labor. His horse was cared for by the others, and his quiet directions were promptly obeyed. The men talked but little, saying that they were from Illinois and were civil engineers looking over the country, to decide upon the feasibility of building more railroads in that section. This party had left Cushman's house at 9 o'clock Thursday morning, and had leisurely ridden the ten miles to Northfield.

THE PURSUIT.

In the meantime there had been mounting in hot haste, and detachments in wagons and on horses had started from Northfield to undertake to head off the bandits on what is known as the Dodd road. This road the robbers seemed to have missed, and, notwithstanding their earlier start, they did not arrive at the town of Shieldsville, fifteen miles away, until after a squad of five men had reached that point. These men were in a saloon refreshing themselves and telling their wonderful tale, when the rough riding marauders dashed up in front of the place. The boys were attracted to the door by the noise of the horses' hoofs, and two or three started for the wagon in which their arms had been left. This movement was promptly checked by the leader, and the lads slouched back to the saloon.

The bandits leisurely proceeded to water their animals, and while doing so an inquisitive old party standing by enquired "where they were going?" All laughed at this query and one, pointing to Bob Younger whose arm was still bleeding, replied that "they were going"

After having watered the horses the desperadoes seemed in no haste, but practiced with their pistols on the pump shattering it to pieces. Soon, however the order was given and all dashed away, going toward Waterville.

The dash and daring of the robbers had electrified the people of the town so that nothing was done, but after they had got well off, the gallant squad of pursuers started on the trail. Soon they were joined by others, augmenting the force to seventeen, and the bandit band was sighted in a ravine about four miles from Shieldsville. The attacking party opened fire from the brow of a hill but their arms consisted of rusty shot guns, and small pistols, hence nothing was accomplished. When the attack commenced the bandits wheeled in platoon and discharged a harmless volley at the pursuers.

The horse of one of the robbers fell, and it was supposed that he had been shot, but he quickly recovered. As the bandit sought to mount him again, he found his girth broken, and in obedience to an order from the chief, he mounted behind his comrade, and the gang moved off at a round trot. The abandoned horse was found to be the one taken from Empey, and the saddle, the one borrowed near Millersburgh.

A BALKY NAG.

An hour or two later the bandits seem to have lost their road, for they called at the house of a farmer named Sager, and demanded a horse, saying they were after horse thieves. Sager is a prudent German, and required to see their authority. They laughed at him and secured his horse, but on attempting to mount him, they found him balky, and were obliged to abandon their plan. They then forced the farmer to accompany them quite a distance to point out the road, first asking the route to Waterville, but finally deciding to take the Cordova road. Sager went with them to the edge of the town of Kilkenny, and left them in a large meadow going towards Cordova.

In this field the bandits resorted to all known means to destroy their tracks, and esconced themselves in the mysterious depths of the Big Woods, where it was impossible to track them, as the thousands of hogs which root up their living there, had almost entirely displaced the sod, and it was not an easy matter to distinguish the footprints of man or beast.

Many have the impression that the bandits were sheltered Thursday night by a notorious character living in the woods on the west side of Kilkenny, but according to the statement of those captured, they lay hidden in the thickets.

THE PURSUIT GROWS HOT.

During Thursday night excited crowds had gathered in all of the towns in the vicinity that could be reached by telegraph. Men of every class volunteered to join in the hunt, and they came armed and mounted in every conceivable style. The great majority had arms of little account, and a large portion of the volunteers were entirely defenceless. There were many intrepid men who joined in the pursuit in an earnest manner, and many younger ones who started as they would in a chicken hunt, for sport and excitement.

The telegrams had summoned the chiefs of police, detectives and several members of the police forces of St. Paul and Minneapolis, and at six o'clock Thursday evening, Chief King, Detective Brissette, Sergeant Clarke and patrolman Brosseau and deputy sheriff Harrison, of the former city, and Chief Munger, Detective Hoy, and officers West, Hankinson, and Shepherd, of the latter place, were on the scene of the tragedy.

Under direction of Chief King, the St. Paul squad followed the trail of the robbers under charge of Detective Brissette, while Detective Hoy and his party proceeded to Faribault intending to start from there and attempt to head off the robber band. Every point of egress from

THE BIG WOODS

was thoroughly picketed during the night, probably two hundred volunteers being engaged. Early on Friday morning Sheriff Asa Barton, of Rice county, who had been up all night arranging the guards, commenced to accept new recruits and dispatch them as rapidly as possible to the front, providing every weapon that would snap a cap, that could be obtained in the vicinity. His labors were arduous and incessant, but his splendid constitution and indomitable perseverance enabled him to endure throughout the three weeks that the hunt continued. The number of robber hunters cannot have been less than five hundred during Friday.

The pursuers dispatched from Faribault were headed by brave, intelligent men, among whom were Col. Williams, J. H. Harding, Dr. Hurd, T. Loyhed, Mr. Baxter, James Hunter and Sam Dunham, chief of police of this city.

Nothing was heard of the bandits during Thursday night, but on Friday, it was found that they had started in a westerly direction. It was difficult to pick their trail, as men and horses shod in every manner had passed over the roads during the night and morning. Rumors of all sorts came in from all points, and the leaders scarcely knew what to do, but they wisely determined to maintain their line of pickets.

It can truly be said that these knights of the road traveled on their reputation, and they were looked upon as such desperate and sanguinary foes that few men would have been willing to meet them except at considerable odds. The pickets had been liberally placed, but the squads were necessarily small, as an area of more than four miles square was guarded. At most places only two or three guards had been placed, and through one of these squads a

WONDERFUL ESCAPE

was made. It was supposed that the bandits would try to break the line at a northerly point, toward Cordova, hence their track to the southwest was unlooked for.

At seven o'clock Friday morning two men called at the house of a Mr. James, on the Cleveland road, and asked his wife, he being away, if she had seen anything of two little black mules that had strayed or been stolen. Being answered in the negative, they asked how far the river was behind the house, and if there were any swamps between. She told them the river was about one-quarter of a mile back, and that there was a swamp which she thought they could pass.

One of the men then inquired which direction was south. Mrs. James informed him, when he said he guessed she was mistaken, but on taking out a pocket compass, he acknowledged that she was correct, and made a polite apology for contradicting her. On leaving, they bade her a pleasant "good morning."

The gang then attempted to cross the Little Cannon river behind James' house but could not get through the swamp, and returning they took to the road going toward Waterville. After proceeding a short distance they accosted a party of five men working on the road. They said they were in pursuit of the robbers, and asked if the two bridges, one above and one below were guarded. When told they were they asked if there were any fords between. On learning that there were two, they said that they had better take care of them, and immediately started across the fields to the river.

No sooner had the bandits left, than Mr. James, who had been told by his wife of the visit of the men, came up. After a hurried consultation, in which it was decided that the party that had just passed were the robbers, James with three of the men hastened to the upper bridge about a quarter of a mile away, and reported to Major Rogers, who with two men held that point. A portion of the squad immediately started for the fords, James and two others going to the lower, while Rogers and the remainder stopped at the upper one about forty rods away.

The swamps and growth had retarded the progress of the bandits, but James had scarcely gained his position when the gang appeared on the opposite bank of the river leading their horses. They were carelessly talking, and made directly for the ford. Just as the leader stepped into the shallow stream, James exclaimed, "Come on boys,"

WE'VE GOT THEM NOW,

at the same time discharging an ineffective charge of small shot at the front robber. At this the leader shouted, "This is too hot, boys, we must take to the woods," and all hastened back up the bank. But as they moved away, they must have heard the retreat of the pickets, who broke and ran, one leaving his time-honored Prussian musket in the brush, and another losing his valuable set of false teeth, for after moving up into the woods for a distance of not more than twenty rods, they wheeled and crossed the ford in the coolest and most deliberate manner. The alarm was immediately carried to Waterville, and the base of operations were soon changed. In the meantime the St. Paul party, with several active and intrepid Northfield men, had been actively on the trail, and just at dusk a sight of the enemy was obtained as they were breaking across a distant cornfield for the cover of the woods.

TRADING HORSES.

But before this the bandits had visited the farm of Ludwig Rosseneau, in Elysian township, and impressed two horses. The farmhouse is entirely secluded from the road, being nearly half a mile back. When the gang arrived there with their five horses, two of them went to the barn, while four remained at a small bridge near by. Mr. Rosseneau and his son went to see what they wanted, when they asked if he had any horses. One said he was the Sheriff of Rice county, and that he must have two horses and a guide, for he was after horse thieves, showing a large document, which the boy Wilhelm, who had been to school, says was a map of Minnesota. When the old man objected, the rascals drew their pistols and quickly closed the bargain. Two horses were brought from the stable and saddled; one was mounted by one of the gang, and the Rosseneau boy was forced to accompany them on the other. The simple German peasants had heard nothing of the Northfield tragedy, and hence were not particularly frightened, although greatly annoyed. The cavalcade passed from the farm, the leader ordering the boy to guide them through the woods to the old state road. It was a difficult country to ride through, but the boy knew the road and traveled along, talking in boyish style and getting short answers, until the chief ordered him not to talk so loud. On arriving at an opening near the road, a halt was made, and the lad was placed upon one of the robbers' horses, which was disabled by a cruel gall caused by the girth under his forelegs. He was told to remain there until they returned, which would be soon. After waiting about half an hour, another lad came up and told him of the robber raid. Young Rosseneau quickly understood his position and made quick tracks for home. He says that after the robbers left him they dashed into the woods across the clearing, and galloped away as fast as possible. The next morning Rosseneau's horses were found in their pasture near the barn.

ANOTHER HORSE TRADE.

Subsequently it was discovered that during the night of Friday a horse had been taken from the pasture of John Laney, 1½ miles from the village of Elysian, and a handsome sorrel mare badly chest foundered placed in its stead for value received. This farmer made a good trade as did Rosseneau, for his own horse came home early Saturday morning.

The hunted bandits were in a country from which it seemed impossible for them to escape, it being almost surrounded by lakes and swamps. A close guard was kept, and all expected that a capture would surely be effected on Saturday. There were hundreds of men on the hunt, but it is useless to say that the search was thorough, for if it had been they would have been found. Saturday passed and also Sunday, and no sign of them was discovered. Many became discouraged and weary, and as the weather had been wet and cold, large numbers of the pursuers returned to their homes.

However, the hunt was continued by many persistant men from all parts of the Stale. As their labor was unrewarded by any discoveries of importance until Monday and Tuesday, the symmetry of the narrative will be maintained by following the robbers according to their own statements.

SAFE FOR AWHILE.

Up to Friday night they had succeeded in procuring food from farm-houses, at one place going in and helping themselves to the entire cooking of the family. Wild plums and grapes had also contributed to their wants, and they had not suffered much, except Bob Younger whose wound was extremely painful. After trading horses at Laney's, Friday night, they rode to a point in the woods about three miles back of Elysian and a short distance from German Lake. Here, less than one hundred and fifty yards from the road, after turning loose the three borrowed horses, they tied their three remaining horses to trees, and made a rude shelter with their rubber blankets in which they passed the night cold and wretched.

Saturday morning they broke camp, and after tying their blankets around themselves with their bridles, they abandoned their faithful steeds, and started forth on foot, leaving five saddles behind them. They moved slowly and cautiously, and during the forenoon they discovered a sort of island which proved an excellent hiding place. In the center of this little-explored tract, they found a pretty pond of water, and feeling secure they established a regular camp, making a good fire, and taking comfort generally. So safe did they feel that they shot a hog and a calf, but not succeeding in killing them the first time, although the shots went straight through their heads as they aver, and as the animals made good time in escaping, they lost a savory feast, not daring to fire more shots. During the most of the time the bandits had proceeded on foot leading their horses through the woods, and their feet had become terribly sore while their stockings were entirely worn out, and while resting here they dressed their

LACERATED EXTREMITIES

and bound them up in socks improvised from their underclothing. But they dared not rest here too long as the corn fields and potato-patches on which they depended for subsistence were at an inconvenient distance, and their hunters might flush their camp at any moment. Saturday night they again took up their tedious march, and about daylight went into camp a mile from the German Catholic church in Marysburgh, the bell of which was plainly heard by the robbers when it rung for early mass. They concluded not to attend church that day, contrary to the usual custom of Cole Younger at least, and a luxurious breakfast of roasted corn and baked potatoes was prepared. This camp was within a few rods of the edge of a clearing, showing the remarkable boldness of the gang. Here two small boys saw three of them walking just outside the woods, and reported it, but little faith was placed on their story, as the general impression was that the bandits were still in the woods behind Elysian or had made a break on their horses to the Minnesota river, and hence to parts unknown. Their camp of Friday night had not then been discovered; and it was supposed that they were still in possession of their horses.

In all the time intervening between Thursday afternoon and Monday morning, the robbers had made but about thirty miles, and although surrounded at times by

AT LEAST FIVE HUNDRED MEN,

they would not have suffered at all except for the cold and rain. In the Sunday camp a portion of a bloody shirt gave evidence that Bob Younger had been compelled to again dress his wounded arm.

Slowly the robbers proceeded, and their next camp was some four miles directly south of Marysburgh on the banks of Lake Madison in Blue Earth county. From here a bold strike was made directly west nearly nine miles, to a point but about 2½ miles back of the city of Mankato, where, finding an empty house in the woods on the Kron farm they slept comfortably Monday and Tuesday nights. During the most of this time they had lived on fodder corn uncooked, hazel nuts, grapes and wild plums, but Tuesday morning they made a requisition on a German farmer and procured a good breakfast. At the table they sat with their overcoats on, and their

BOWIE KNIVES BY THEIR PLATES.

They were uncommunicative, inoffensive and polite, and paid liberally for the hospitality shown them.

The hunt had continued while the bandits were escaping as above related, a reward of $1,000 offered by Governor Pillsbury, $700 by the Northfield bank, and $500 by the Winona and St. Peter railroad inciting many to action. The state reward was afterwards increased to $1,000 for each man dead or alive. However all were off the scent, the objective point of the pursuers being the woods back of Elysian from which the pursued had quietly passed. The headquarters of the robber hunters were made

AT JANESVILLE.

On Saturday, Sept. 9th, a party consisting of A. A. Keller, Russell M. Church, F. Martin and W. Rhine started across the country from Northfield to Faribault, and catching there the train, proceeded to Owatonna, where they were joined by a party of some thirty well armed citizens.

Telegrams were sent to Waseca for a special train to carry them to Janesville. Finding a case of needle guns at Owatonna for Brisette, they took them on with them, arriving at Janesville at one o'clock. They found Brisette and his men there. They had been on the track of the gang from the first, often getting sight of them, and never for an hour losing their trail till Saturday, when they failed to see them during the whole day.

Early in the morning the party was divided into companies and took to the woods, determined to hunt the villains up. Besides the parties sent out in squads to the woods, other parties were out in each direction up the Winona and St. Peter R. R. on hand cars.

The whole country around Janesville was alive, and hundreds of volunteers were rushing about in search of arms to join the pursuers. By noon on Sunday there were at least three hundred men on the war-path, seeking for the fugitives and anxious to secure some portion of the reward offered for their capture.

The telegraph was kept in lively operation, and every rumor was sent from point to point, and mounted messengers carried the news along the lines of outposts, keeping the men well informed on the events of the day.

At about 3 o'clock a messenger came riding up to headquarters, his horse reeking and foaming, and the man's manner portending news of the utmost weight and importance. Hurrying in to the depot he handed the telegraph operator a paper containing the information that the fugitives broke cover near Elysian and were making for Waterville. To inquiries he answered that three of the robbers were seen and one was riding a cream-colored horse, and that the police were hard on their track.

Telegrams were at once sent to Eagle Lake, Owatonna, and other points, repeating the exciting tale and asking that the posts along the line between Waseca and Janesville be made especially strong—the supposition being that the thieves would try to cross somewhere between those two points. In prompt reply to these telegrams a special train was dispatched containing over one hundred men, well-armed, from Northfield, Winona, Rochester, Owatonna and Medford, and these were left in squads often between Waseca and Janesville, twenty-two of them coming up for instructions and news.

These twenty-two were under the command of C. Runnels. Many were

VETERANS OF THE WAR,

and they seemed to be under good discipline, all obeying their leader's orders with alacrity. This party it was thought better to use as a company of patrol, who were to visit the outposts between this section and Waseca.

THE ST. PAUL POLICE

and the five Northfield scouts came in about 9:30 o'clock Saturday night, and to the surprise of numbers of people waiting for news, reported that they had no news to tell. They knew nothing of the dispatch which had awakened such lively interest.

The party had been out all day, having left Janesville at 8 o'clock with four wagons and some on horseback. They proceeded first to Elysian and passing round the lake then proceeded on to Marysburg, within four miles of which they fell in with Hoy and

THE MINNEAPOLIS POLICE,

when all started by different routes to Eagle Lake, from thence they came to Janesville after spending twelve long hours on the road, but throughout their whole course they saw and heard nothing of the robbers.

Subsequent developments proved that the news brought in by the mounted messenger was a canard founded on the fact that some of the robber hunters had been amusing themselves by "playing robbers." The false alarm, however, did no harm, and only stirred men to double diligence, and the writer who spent the whole night of Sunday in visiting the outposts and guards along the Winona & St. Peter railroad found them all on the *qui vive*, and he is confident if the bandits had shown themselves that night, they would have fared badly.

The alarm telegraphed to St. Paul brought out again Chief King and another body of police and citizens among whom was Hazen, of Cincinnati, who thought he recognized in photographs of the two dead bandits, Bill Chadwell and Charles Pitts.

FINDING THE HORSES.

Monday night, a party, headed by Sheriff Dill and Brissette, and including the St. Paul police, and several determined men from Northfield, after a tedious hunt arrived at the house of John Dehn about a mile from the place where Brisette had lost the trail on Friday night.

The detective was in a quandary not understanding how the horses at least could have got through the line of pickets that had been maintained. One of these animals was of a dun color, or as the country people called it "a yaller hoss," and would have been noticed among a cavalry regiment.

The mystery was soon to be solved however. A portion of the squad took refuge in Dehn's hay loft for the night, and at daylight Tuesday morning as Mr. Mills Church, of Northfield, an old war veteran, was peeping from his roost, he saw two hard looking horses, peering over the farm gate, evidently envying the inviting stack of oats within.

Church immediately went to them, and found they were two of the robbers' horses without doubt. One was a bright bay with white face and three white feet, and the other was a handsome brown mare. Both were very thin and showed marks of exposure, and deep rowelling on their sides. The brown had large galls each side of her back bone made by the saddle, and these were covered by thick scabs that had been forming at least three days. Both wore halters, that of the bay being without a strap, while a piece about a foot long hung to the halter of the brown, it having been chewed off by the wearer.

The nags were well cared for, and their trail was immediately taken up while their tracks were fresh, but the horses had stopped to graze so often thus doubling and changing their course, that it was almost a fruitless task. Feeling that Dehn's house at which they were found was probably the first one the horses saw, a

LONG LINE OF SKIRMISHERS

was formed, and a thorough search of the woods made. At about 7 o'clock the left of the line came upon the last camp where the robbers were in possession of their horses. Dr. Hurd of Faribault was in advance, and as he came to the spot, the noted buckskin horse whinned and stamped showing most unmistakable signs of delight at again seeing a human form. The camp was located so near the road that it is a wonder that it had not been discovered. At each of three saplings a horse had been tied, the yellow one in the middle. They had been given as long range as possible, but there was no feed for them except the bark and wood of the trees to which they were tied. These were eaten as high as the horses could reach and deep into the roots. The ground around was stamped hard, and there were evidences that the poor animals had made desperate efforts to escape. At a short distance away pronged stakes were found which showed that the fleeing men had found shelter in a most uncomfortable manner. They had probably thrown blankets over the frame and stopped to dress the wounded man. There was no trace of eating or sleeping. Behind a log near by, all the saddles of the five laid in a pile, an old russet-leather saddle, much defaced, at the bottom of the pile, very wet. This showed two shot marks, from one of which a medium-sized pistol bullet was taken. Two others on the pile were black, solid-seat saddles, one new, open, black McClellan, one new russet McClellan. The black McClellan was marked underneath, at the front, $8.50, with the cost mark above: two old blankets and three old gunny bags were found. The robbers carried away all the bridles and good blankets.

The horses at Rosseneau's and Laney's were then procured and the entire five were delivered to Commissioner Scott of Rice county, it being the feeling that that community should have the benefit of what was recovered.

EXCITING NEWS.

Excitement had again subsided, and after the capture of the robbers' horses in a state indicating that they had been abandoned for several days, the opinion gained ground rapidly that the robbers had made tracks on foot and were many miles away. The hunt had virtually come to an end, was the thought of many, and a general movement was made by the pursuers toward those homes to which of late, they had become strangers. The St. Paul police had started for home, and the Minneapolis force was already there. The indefatigable and energetic sheriff of Winona, was even contemplating an abandonment of the chase when news was brought into Mankato, which at once aroused excitement to its highest pitch. A farmer had been captured by the bandits, and with arms tightly bound behind him, compelled at the muzzle of a revolver to accompany them on the road to pilot the way beyond Mankato. Hearing that this unfortunate was the man in charge of Mr. Shaubut's farm, the writer sought out the man

DUNNING,

who told him that about six o'clock on Wednesday morning the 13th, he started from his house in search of the cows. He had scarcely passed the barn going towards the woods when six men came upon him. They were for the most part powerfully built men, well dressed, with linen dusters and blankets strapped up in bridles. The men came up to him and said they were

LOOKING FOR ROBBERS,

and guessed he was one of them. He protested that he was not, when one said they would take him with them anyhow, and proceeded to bind his hands behind him with a bridle rein. They then insisted, upon his showing them the way past Mankato, so that they might strike the Minnesota above, asking him questions as to whether they would be likely to find any boats upon the river, and if it was possible to ford or swim across. Dunning begged them to let him go, when they told him they were

THE NORTHFIELD ROBBERS,

but if he would show them the way and keep a silent tongue in his head they would send him a handsome present. He still begged to be released, stating that he had a delicate wife and young children, and if he should be away from the farm he would lose his situation, and then what would his family do during the winter? The robbers thought he seemed a good sort of a fellow, and if they could only trust him, perhaps they might let him return, but could they trust him? Dunning protested by all that was sacred that they might, and promised if they would only let him return home, he would not breathe to a living soul that he had seen there and he expressed a hope that they would get through safe and sound without being captured. The robbers held a short consultation among themselves, in which Dunning thought he heard proposals of shooting him on the spot. It was to him

A MOMENT OF DREADFUL SUSPENSE,

and he shook with very fear, but to his inexpressible relief one of the men said that they had agreed to let him return home—they did not want his family to suffer for them. They then asked him his name and postal address, which they carefully noted down, repeating their former promise of a handsome present if they got safely off, and if he kept his faith with them.

One of the men asked if they could not get to the river from where they were by leaving the timber and crossing the level open flat, and if they could not swim the river easily. To which Dunning replied that they would be discovered almost immediately if they attempted to leave the woods, advising them to keep under cover as much as they could. With this they released his arms and set him free, they the while seating themselves upon the ground and watching him till he got out of sight. He at once ran home, and after getting his breakfast, he crossed over from his house to the residence of Mr. Shaubut, and told him the whole story.

MR. SHAUBUT,

who is a banker in Mankato, brought the news to town, which set the whole city into commotion. Men of all classes hurried about for arms. The telegraph wires called up from Janesville the few men who still lingered there reluctant to give up the chase. The same lightning messenger brought men from Winona, Waseca, Owatonna, and Faribault. St. Peter, and Le Sueur sent in their quota of armed citizens. The message found the redoubtable Hoy at the Nicollet hotel, where he was narrating to an admiring throng his exploits at Elysian, and brought him back to the regained trail; the same message arrested the St. Paul police on their homeward journey at Blakely, and, in an incredibly short time

A THOUSAND EAGER HUNTERS

crowded into the streets of Mankato seeking information and anxious for orders. The ubiquitous Dill was there with his disciplined men. Baxter was there and Sheriffs Finch, Davis, Barton, Long and Harrison, Mayor Wiswell and Captains Holmes and Owens. Thus were the counties of Winona, Blue Earth, Rice, Waseca, Faribault and Ramsey represented by their sheriffs and men. The five Northfield boys, who had never for an hour given up the hunt, were there and ready again to guard, mount and scour the woods.

Davis, of Winnebago, whose story of the robbers' appearance the evening before at Indian Lake, was so little heeded, was now almost lionized, and it was surprising how many were all at once found who believed in the famous horse thief catcher from the first.

It was necessary that some system be pursued; accordingly General Pope, of Mankato, was appointed generalissimo of the forces, and that gentleman at once set about a plan of organization. Bridges must be guarded, cross-roads and by-paths watched, patrols sent out, and skirmish lines established. One would think by the measured tramp of armed men, the bustle, the eager excitement, the groups of mysterious gossips, that Mankato expected a seige from the combined forces of all the hostile savages paying allegiance to Sitting Bull, rather than that the men were called out to capture six fugitive robbers.

But the people seemed determined. Their looks seemed to say that they were tired of playing this game of hide and seek, and were for once in downright earnest and bent upon bringing this thing to a quick and decisive close.

It was a miserably wet morning, the rain descending in a continuous shower, and the air was filled with a damp chilliness, which rendered out-door vocations particularly disagreeable. The streets and roads were filled with slimy mud—griming and sticking, to the intense misery of pedestrians. But the rain and the mud and the cold could not deter the excited populace, and even women caught the infectious fever of excitement and dared the elements in search of news. All the city was on the tip-toe of expectancy, but the hours glided slowly along and no news was brought in from the skirmish lines or outposts. Reports, it is true, were rife, and many a thrilling tale of manly courage and sanguinary encounter was whispered by mani-tongued rumor. At one time the robbers were all slaughtered, at another, a brave citizen was sacrificed, but enquiry proved them to owe their existence to fertile imaginations. Evening at last closed in upon a miserable day, and the tired, wet and hungry hunters began to return. The Clifton house was filled with them, the congenial host doing his best to appease their ravenous appetites, after which the weary men stretched themselves at length upon the floors of the parlors, offices and halls to snatch a few minutes' refreshing slumber. Meantime a strong guard was placed at every point around the city, and mounted men patrolled the streets all night.

At about midnight some of the men on guard heard peculiar whistles at different points, which seemed to be replied to, the call resembling the low note of the quail, and the answer, the high note of the same bird. Report was made of the circumstance at "Headquarters," and while a discussion was progressing as to whether the men were not mistaken, and their ability to distinguish between the veritable bird call and its its imitation, a mounted messenger came dashing in with the news that three of the robbers had

CROSSED THE BRIDGE,

over the Blue Earth river and had escaped toward South Bend. The news spread like a prairie fire, and in an incredibly short time the streets were alive with armed men hastening down toward the point at which the fugitives had broken the line of outposts. Sheriff Dill, who, had retired but a few minutes to the well-deserved comfortable bed put at his disposal at the Clifton, was soon up and away with a posse of men. Other leaders were equally alert, but all mentally, and some physically, too, cursed the blundering guard, which had permitted itself to be caught napping. Enquiry soon ascertained the fact that

SOME ONE HAD BLUNDERED.

It appears that General Pope in arranging for the night guard had provided for a strong body of men being placed upon each of the bridges over the Blue Earth, this being considered the vulnerable point in the line, but a telegram coming to him stating that the railroad bridge would be specially guarded by the railroad officials, he removed his guard from that structure, and, as it proved, opened a direct way for the brigands' escape. The railroad authorities had placed two men and a boy on the bridge to guard it, and about two o'clock they saw three men approaching in single file. The guard stood on one side and the men advanced and walked deliberately on to the trestle work and passed over, the heroic guard being too much frightened to even breathe. As soon as the fugitives had got fairly past, the boy rushed down to the covered bridge and alarmed the guard there, who at once sent a mounted messenger into the city to tell the miserable tale. Nothing during the whole hunt had such a humiliating effect upon the people as this fiasco, but they were doomed ere long to receive as great a disappointment.

The night was one of almost Egyptian darkness, and men could do little good tramping through muddy lanes and through dripping woods without a trail to guide them. The resolve, therefore, was to await the break of day, when at the earliest hour of dawn a close hunt and hot pursuit would commence. Accordingly with the gloaming, Hoy, of Minneapolis, with a number of Mankato men and others, started out and they were soon shown

A TRAIL

which led across the railroad bridge along the Sioux City line into a melon patch, back to the road and on across the Garden City road. The engineer of an incoming train motioned the pursuers toward the thick woods covering the slopes of Pigeon Hill, some two hundred yards from the State road. But on went the chattering, noisy trail-hunters, chasing each other up the line. Quickly they came to a halt and found they had overrun the trail. Doubling upon their tracks they came back several yards and found the foot-prints turned off into the woods. Their attention was now attracted by a strong smell of burning feathers, and looking up toward the beautifully wooded acclivity, they saw a thin, pale column of smoke issuing from the luxurious foliage and spreading itself out like a hazy film.

At this point there seems to be conflicting statements as to what was done, some asserting that Hoy at once made a dash toward the campfire; others say that he spent several minutes consulting and ordering his own men back to Garden City road to surround the camp. One man, Mr. Hansen, of Mankato, says that he actually saw one of the robbers and wanted to fire, but Hoy would not let him, stating that he might hit some of the pursuers instead of the pursued. Both Cole and Bob Younger afterward stated that Hoy did not charge into the camp at all. Be this as it may, the camp when entered was found to be deserted. When the writer entered the

ROBBER'S CAMP,

a bright, clear fire was burning, in front of which, toward the railroad, a long pole was wedged in between some saplings, over which had been hung the coats and blankets of the band. The front part of a shirt was found, stained with blood. One wristband was wanting, but that found at the camp discovered on the previous Sunday, exactly corresponded with it. The shirt was of good quality and had evidently never been laundried. Bob Younger afterwards told the writer that the garment belonged to him. A blood-stained handkerchief (new) with border torn from two sides was found, with a large blue weather-proof coat, a brown linen duster, nearly new, a piece of drugget about two yards square and two bridles. One of the bridles had a very severe Mexican bit, and was afterwards recognized by a Mankato man as being one that he had exchanged at St. Peter for a milder one. Near the fire were two fowls and a chicken skillfully dressed and jointed ready for broiling, and several cobs of corn, some of it partially roasted, and some of it showing marks of teeth, as though some of the men were too hungry to wait till breakfast was ready. At the back of the camp fire the hill ascended precipitously, and in the dead leaves were distinctly seen the trail of the disturbed bandits. Reaching the summit of Pigeon Hill, they crossed the Garden City road and entered the heavy timber and dense underbrush leading down to the Blue Earth river. The whole of this wood was filled with men, a party of about two hundred men forming a skirmish line about three paces apart and marching completely through it down to Jones' ford. It was now about mid-day, and it was thought the outlaws had doubled on their track and were concealed somewhere in the thick coverts of

BEAUTIFUL MINNEOPA.

Accordingly toward this lovely spot were the forces concentrated, and all the afternoon the wide space fronting the Rev. D. T. Rowland's residence was filled with armed men. Although this delightful spot is well known to pleasure-seekers, it is doubtful if ever before it was the scene of so much bustle and animation, and the two beautiful daughters of the reverend gentleman were kept busily employed attending to the wants of their countless guests.

The whole neighborhood was thoroughly searched, the deep and shadowing glen, the rocky chasms, the towering heights were all searched through and through, not a thicket nor a cave, nor a gloomy recess in the tortuous course of the serpentine Minneinneopa escaped the ruthless tread of the pursuers. No one could form an adequate idea of the number of men engaged in the hunt if they remained themselves with one party or in one place. As the writer was taken from one point to another, along highways and by ways by a spirited span of colts, supplied by Mr. B. D. Pay, he was astonished at the number of skirmishers he met. There were men of

ALL AGES AND ALL NATIONALITIES,

mounted and on foot, shadowed by every tree and covered by every bush. Could it be possible for an escape through such a formidable line!

Driving up from Rush Lake towards evening weary and hungry from the day's exertion, the writer was hailed by three men hastening across from heavy timber to the right of the Garden City road. Halting, he was told excitedly that the three men crossing from Garden City came upon a dense thicket overhanging the Blue Earth river where they heard voices. They stopped and listened when they distinctly heard a voice.

"There is a good shelter here, why should we move."

It was raining at the time. The men from Garden City waited and watched, but they saw nothing. After some time they fired off their shot guns, but no response was made. For four hours the men kept guard over the place, and as night was coming on they thought they would go out in search of help.

The writer at once alighted from his buggy and being joined by some dozen armed men, they approached the spot indicated. The cover was almost impenetrably dense, and it was impossible to see a dozen yards in any direction, and the hunt ended in failure, some of the party believing that the three men from Garden city had given way to a strong imagination. But at

AN INTERVIEW WITH THE YOUNGERS,

at Madelia, the writer was told that after leaving the camp at Minneopa Falls, the band went in a south-easterly direction to the Blue Earth, and then followed up the river for half an hour where they lay in a dense thicket all day. The men in concealment heard the pursuers, heard the shots, and saw one at least of the party within easy pistol range of them. At nightfall many of the hunters returned to Mankato, but still more remained out all night performing picket duty after an arduous day's march through the woods and over a rough country.

THE LINE ADVANCED.

The search of Thursday having proved fruitless, as night approached the line was thrown some five miles in advance due west, and a cordon of pickets was stretched from Judson, on the Minnesota river, to Garden City, on the Watonwan river, a distance of at least thirteen miles. The line passed through the village of Lake Crystal, the pickets being liberally disposed at all of the roads, crossings, fords and ferries. Brissette, Harrison and Clark, aided by W. Erwin, of St. Paul, (a most admirable organizer and active commander,) and Baxter, of Faribault, having charge of the arrangements, and acting under the orders of Gen. Pope, who had changed his headquarters to Lake Crystal. The town board of that place responded with the most commendable promptitude to every expressed desire of the leaders, providing provisions for a large number of men and horses, and furnishing transportation for the pickets to their several locations.

At an early hour in the evening the picketing was completed, and the commander-in-chief with his aids watched through the night, momentarily expecting the arrival of

COURIERS WITH NEWS,

everything being arranged to mass a great number of men at any point from which tidings of the bandits should be received. Shortly after midnight startling news was brought in, and it transpired that the wily bandits had again selected the weakest place in the line, and succeeded in passing a stupid crowd of sleepy pickets.

A NEW DEPARTURE

ANOTHER ESCAPE.

It appears that at a crossing over a small creek on the outskirts of Lake Crystal, ten guards had been placed. Nine of them had procured hay and ensconced themselves in the bushes to enjoy a quiet sleep. A young man named Richard Roberts, of Mankato, alone was faithful to his trust, and while the others slept he kept his ceaseless vigil. The night was pitchy dark, but the brave boy had become accustomed to it, and his ear was rendered wonderfully acute. At about midnight he thought he heard the sound of horse's hoofs on the deep sand of the road, and he got a position where if any one passed he could read the outlines against the sky. Soon a horse appeared bearing two riders.

Stepping from his bush he cried "halt," when the two men slid over to the further side of the horse. Dick then raised his rifle, and as the bandits undertook to rush their horse past him, he fired. The animal gave a start, throwing his riders, and ran rapidly away.

The two men must have been hit in the legs, but they were not disabled, for they immediately gained their feet and dashed into a cornfield near by, where their trail was lost until morning. In falling they made deep indentions in the sand, and one lost his hat, which was of fine make and nearly new. Before young Roberts had time to start in pursuit, the frightened horse again dashed by him in hot haste to his home about two miles back. Early in the morning of Friday a farmer named John Vincent came into town, and reported that one of his horses had been used by the robbers during the night.

BORROWING A HORSE.

All of the farmers in the vicinity had been warned to take the strictest care of their horses for fear that the robbers would appropriate them. In accordance with these suggestions Mr. Vincent had turned his horses into a concealed meadow, and locked his barn strongly, after removing all except his cart harness to the house. However, the cunning robbers found the animal, and breaking into the barn improvised a bridle with a halter and an old bit, cutting the long lines of the cart harness for reins, girth and stirrups. The next morning the poor old black horse, which bore an admirable reputation for honesty, was found meekly standing in the door yard evidently ashamed of the Tam O'Shanter ride in which he had assisted. He was dirty, and lame, and his sides bled from the wounds inflicted by the cruel spurs of the bandits.

ON THE NEW TRAIL.

A large number of hunters were soon on the scene of the affair and efforts were made to follow the trail with lanterns, but nothing was accomplished except to establish the identity of the robbers by the impress of a boot leaving a

SMALL HEEL AND SQUARE TOE,

and which had been the guiding mark wherever the trail had been struck. At daylight the trail was found by the impatient hunters, and it was rapidly followed to the Seymour farm about four miles away across the fields. Here the fleeing villains had unceremoniously helped themselves to a splendid team of large gray mares, owned by Geo. Rockwood, who was engaged in haying on the farm. These animals were reputed to be the best in the county, and their subsequent achievements proved that their reputation was merited. The robbers had appropriated bridles, but finding no saddles they proceeded, riding bareback. It is supposed that they stole these horses at about three o'clock Friday morning, and it was nearly six o'clock before it became known, so that pursuit could be organized.

Couriers were dispatched to recall the pickets, and no time was lost in arranging a pursuit.

BREAKFAST AND A HAT.

Soon news arrived by telegraph that the robbers had called at the house of a farmer named Jackson, two miles northwest of Madelia, at 6 o'clock, and asked for something to eat. On being told that breakfast was not ready, and urged to dismount and wait for it, they said they did not want breakfast, only a loaf of bread. The good wife gave them what they asked for, and they insisted upon paying for it. Mrs. Jackson finally accepted ten cents.

One of the visitors was hatless, and he asked if they could not provide him with an old one, as his had blown off into a swamp. Mrs. Jackson said that they had only a new one which she had bought for her son the day before. This the robber persuaded her to sell him for $1.50, and then both started off at a brisk pace.

At 1:30 p. m., the fugitives called at the farm of Andrew Nelson, four miles directly west of Madelia, and asked a few questions in regard to the roads, and at two o'clock they called at another house on the same errand. They made excellent headway, for later in the afternoon they were seen near Mountain Lake, some seventeen miles from Madelia. The alarm had been flashed ahead over the wires, and squads were turning out from all points in hot pursuit.

CAVALRY RAID BY RAILROAD.

As soon as possible a special train consisting of an engine and two box-cars was dispatched to Lake Crystal and placed at the disposal of Gen. Pope, by the active and accommodating manager of the Sioux City railroad. Two squads of eight carefully chosen men each were detailed to proceed under command of Sheriff Barton, of Rice county, and Detective Hoy, of Minneapolis. Barton's detachment transported eight horses, but Hoy decided to rely upon the farmers for his stock. The former went directly to Windom, and the latter to Mountain Lake, from which points they started north, hoping to intercept the robbers. However, their efforts were futile, as it was subsequently learned that the desperadoes had passed, and were headed in a northwesterly direction.

ON THE BOUNDLESS PRAIRIE.

On the evening of Friday, the railroad was again resorted to and a squad was dispatched to a point certainly in advance of the bandits, hoping to arouse the inhabitants away from the railroad and telegraph. On the train was Sheriff McDonald, of Woodbury county, Dakota territory, and it was arranged between him and Sheriff Dill, who led the squad, that he should proceed immediately to Sioux City, organize two squads, and make for Sioux Falls by two routes. An account of the last days of the hunt for these two fugitives in this State will be found in the following special telegram forwarded by the writer to the St. Paul *Pioneer-Press*.

THREE DAYS' HUNT.

"I took the train for Heron Like, with Sheriff Dill and ten men, including Brissette, Clark, Harrison, Brosseau, Gail, Avery, Richardson and Church. Arrived there at 11:30, roused the inhabitants, and were soon under way in teams for Lake Shetek. The citizens were eager to assist and ready to go to the front. At sunrise took a farmer's family by surprise, but got a good breakfast, our tired squad tumbling into warm beds. We were left by the inmates of the house to sleep an hour and a half, and then started, feeling better for a chicken stew. Reached the town of Currie, Lake Shetek township, at noon. Traveled in heavy farm wagons over bad roads. Here found the little community ready to assist in any way. Our theory was that the robbers would take"

ONE OF THREE TRAILS PASSING BETWEEN

Shetek and Luverne, and on the way out left six pickets to guard the lower trails—Brissette, Clark and Brosseau, one squad; three Winona men another; Erwin and Harrison were mounted well and served as scouts. It was thought that the most likely course for the robbers was by the upper trail, hence the scouts accompanied the commander, in order to communicate with the pickets eight and five miles below. Dill quickly found men at his disposal, and soon had twenty pickets posted north and south. Just at night Erwin and Harrison dashed in and reported that the robbers had called at the house of Mr. Swan, at the crossing of the Des Moines river, Lime Creek township, five miles south of Shetek, at two. This was on Saturday. There was only a woman at the house. The description of the outlaws was accurate. They were still on the gray horses, stolen near Lake Crystal. They did not get off their horses, and asked for bread. The woman asked them to come in, but they declined, and after they got bread and milk, they asked for meat. They said they were after horse-thieves, and started southwest. Later they were seen at the Lutheran church, in the town of Center, Murray township, from which point they went southwest, striking the

LAST HOUSE ON THE FRONTIER

at section twenty-two, town one hundred and six, range forty-one, at 4:30. They were tracked here by Avery, Gail and Richardson, of Winona, and a courier brought the news to the scouts. This news caused Dill to decide that they were making for the "Lost Timber," a natural hiding place.

Recruits were called for and couriers dispatched to call in the pickets in other directions, to concentrate on that point. A squad consisting of thirty was raised, ten being mounted. No time was lost, and through the cold, dismal night,

A FORCED MARCH

was made to Lowville, where we arrived in a big thunder storm, at one, Sunday morning. Rested here for a hot lunch at Bartlett Low's until five o'clock, when the extra horsemen started across the broad prairie to the famous "Lost Timber," which it was calculated was in advance of the robbers, as it was supposed they must rest after their superhuman efforts. The roads were heavy. We reached the destination at ten, and found Erwin and Harrison with six riders, who had been skirmishing all night at the spot, and had established

CAMP COLE YOUNGER.

They had picketed their horses in a deep ravine, and deployed men on the row of high mounds commanding the prairie, and five miles down "Lost Timber" valley. On arriving there, Dill's pickets were carried out three miles each way, and a watch kept for four hours. Scouts were sent down the valley, and and the pockets or ravines examined. At two p. m., no tidings being received, a council was held, and it was agreed that the robbers must have changed their route. Dill had been sanguine in regard to the Luverne route, and he, Church of Northfield, and I took a team for that point, leaving most of the party to push on to Pipestone, on the northern trail, knowing plenty of men could be started from Luverne. A ride of twenty tedious miles brought us to this point at 7:30 p. m. Found the town in an uproar of excitement, as news had been sent from Worthington and a special train dispatched with twenty men to guard the trail passing the town. About noon Sunday, a man named Rolfe, living eleven miles north of town, on the west bank of Rock river, came in and reported, that at 7:30 while he was away from the house, two men called at his house and asked for breakfast. They got off their gray horses, and went into the house. The woman asked them to take off their rubber coats. They refused to do so, and seemed very lame, and shuffled along,

UNABLE TO LIFT THEIR LEGS.

Mrs. Rolfe asked if they were sick. One said their horses had ran away and broke the wagon on the prairie, and they were forced to take to horse. He said he had got the rheumatism and his comrade had broken two ribs in falling from the wagon. This one gave evidence of a bad wound in the right side, and could scarcely sit up to eat breakfast. He refused tea and asked for milk. When they paid for their breakfast they did not unbutton their coats, but reached up under. It took a long time to mount, and they had to climb upon the fence and slide on to their horses. Both wore rubber coats, one torn on the right side, and one had fine boots with small heel and square toes. The boots were red from walking through the grass. They had bags filled with straw for saddles, and old ropes looped for stirrups. They moved slowly away southward. The robbers stopped at the house of Davis, in Springwater, and were given bread and butter. They staid fifteen minutes. From here they crossed the road northward from Luverne. As these reports came in, the citizens were roused and the

PURSUIT WAS HOT.

They had been noticed by parties driving into town. At three they were seen by Mr. Howard, who thought they were pleasure riders. They drove on a high knoll and surveyed the country then traveled on at a moderate gait. Shortly after, Sheriff Rice and three others in pursuit came very near them, so they could have reached them with their rifles, but were

AFRAID OF THEM,

and were blamed for not shooting. This party followed seven miles without attacking, and lost the trail after dark, three miles east of the Palisades, on Splitrock river, in Dakota. About half an hour after, Rice met a boy who said they had passed, and told him some fellows were following, giving him

A VULGAR INVITATION

to report to the pursuers. They evidently felt easy, as they were in familiar territory, and asked the boy where they could cross the river. He directed them to two crossings, and they started towards the lower, but had not crossed at six. They were in a country hard to hunt, full of knolls and ravines. The stage from Sioux Falls this afternoon brought in the two gray horses, which were found at the house of Mr. Nelson, on Splitrock river, below the Palisades. The robbers called there between six and eight o'clock Sunday evening. Kelson lit a pipe and sat on the fence talking. One robber asked if he was

GOING TO SIT THERE ALL NIGHT,

and inquired about the fords and roads. After Nelson went in, the outlaws changed their grays for his two horses, both black and blind, one in both eyes, and the other in one. Nelson saw their revolvers. They rode the blacks until two o'clock Monday morning, but made only ten miles, when they changed for a pair of grays, five miles north of Sioux Falls. The blind horses probably did not suit them. They went through Sioux Falls about five Monday morning, and overtook the Yankton stage. They asked the driver where he was going. The driver told them, and asked them the same question. The robbers did not answer, but turned back into Sioux Falls. This is

THE LAST SEEN

of the two supposed to be the James brothers, as far as known in this State. Their course has been almost directly west by compass. I think they would have taken the northern trail, but were driven south by Dill's division in that direction. The fugitives were robbed of rest they intended to take, and were forced to make eighty miles without stopping, thus showing that they had good horses.

Various reports have been received recently in regard to the escaped bandits, but they are probably safely away and among their old familiar scenes.

A few determined spirits followed into Dakota, but the great body of the pursuers returned disappointed to their homes, and resumed their avocations, only to be again stirred and inspired in a few days by the remarkable events which will be found in the succeeding chapter.

THE CAPTURE.

"WHAT'S THE USE?"

was the bitter ejaculation of pretty well every man who had for two long weeks persistently kept on the trail of the gang of desperadoes who perpetrated the Northfield outrage, and by Wednesday evening, the 20th, the pursuers had for the most part returned to their homes with the full conviction that the chase was up, and the bandits had made good their escape. To some it was more than humiliating that after so many times being completely within their grasp, the scoundrels had succeeded in eluding them, and this too, so often through blundering and neglect. It seemed no consolation that the robbers had lost more in the State than they had ever done elsewhere. The two dead carcasses at Northfield, the captured horses, the wounded, fleeing men were impotent to assuage their disappointment and heal their wounded pride.

Many exciting reports came from all quarters, but they were only met with incredulous laughter. The bandits were gone, and that was an end to the matter. People began to look upon the whole hunt as a huge joke, and admiration soon showed itself for the plucky six who could in the face of such fearful odds make good their escape. But there were those who still thought that at least four of the robbers were still in the neighborhood— the man wounded at Northfield, and the three who had not crossed the river, for notwithstanding the fact that J. Devans, of South Bend, said that he saw *five* men in South Bend, whom he was positive were the robbers, on the morning that the three crossed the bridge, no one gave credence to his tale.

This man asserted that he had occasion to get up about half-past two o'clock to get some water at the pump, his wife being sick, when he passed five men in the lane near South Bend Hotel. They wore long linen dusters with belts, and carried blankets done up in bridles, and he was positive they were the robbers. He saw them leave and go on to the railroad, two walking ahead, and the fifth man who was taller than the others, walking behind and seeming to stoop greatly and walk with difficulty, carrying one arm in a sling. Bob Younger's statement to the writer seemed to confirm Devan's story.

There were not a few people in Mankato who believed that Jack O'Neil had a hand in the escape of the raiders. It will be remembered that this man figured conspicuously as an informant in a case spoken of at an early period of this narrative. Rumor had it that this O'Niel had still in his vicious den the wounded man concealed. To satisfy the public mind, a strong body of men crossed over the ferry and thoroughly searched O'Niel's premises in which were found, besides the unfortunate female denizens, five as low looking vagabonds as were ever seen outside of prison walls. Although the search was fruitless, there are many people in Mankato who still think, now that the hunt is over, that the notorious Jack cleared his house of Ingalls, Peabody and Quane, because he expected the Northfield raiders on their return trip to stay and make use of his house. Many arrests were made of innocent persons in the eagerness to catch the robbers, and it was absolutely dangerous to be a large man of unusual appearance, especially to be alone in the woods or on country roads. There was one instance of a capture on suspicion which placed two horse thieves within the grasp of inexorable justice, that of the capture of the two men at St. Peter, who stayed at the old Wardlow place one night and rode off suspiciously at an early hour of the morning. These men who gave their names as John Chafer and George Ranks, proved to be two horse thieves from Iowa.

But the hunt was at last given up in despair and people had gone back to their homes, when a lad came dashing into Madelia shouting out to every one he met, that the

ROBBERS WERE FOUND.

Exhausted and out of breath from his long and rapid ride, it was some few moments ere he could sufficiently recover himself to tell an intelligent story. To Col. Vought, the landlord of the Flanders Hotel, the boy gave his statement.

The following is condensed from the sworn statement of the captors, and was published in the *"Madelia Times:"*

Early on Thursday morning, September 21st, a Norwegian boy named Oscar O. Suborn, while out milking, saw two men pass his father's house. This boy lives eight miles from this place in a direction a little west of north, in Linden township, Brown county. In a few moments, he set down his pail and went to the house of Mads Ouren, and told what he had seen. Besides Mr. Ouren, there were there, Anton Anderson, Ole Stone and J. F. Devine. The latter said at once he believed it was the robbers, and that the people should be notified. Those there proceeded at once to do so. A gang were commencing to thresh nearby, so their horses and all others in the vicinity were ran off as fast as possible. The boy returned home and was there told that during his absence, the two other men had come to the house and called for something to eat. Said they were a fishing party, were in a hurry and could not stop for breakfast. The boy then jumped upon his father's horse and came full speed to this place with the news. When within a mile and a half of town, his horse fell down and threw him off into the mud, but he re-mounted and hastened on. Arriving here, the first he saw were Sheriff Glispin and T. L. Vought. The latter grasped his gun, mounted his horse and was off, closely followed by J. Severson. They were soon joined by Sheriff Glispin, after having left orders to others to come, and Will Estes. About three or four miles out they were met by a young man named Flittie, who

HAD SEEN THE ROBBERS

and guided them to where the villains were. When the party came in sight of the robbers, the latter were at the house of John Sharphold. Seeing their pursuers coming they seemed to try to fortify behind a heap of earth, but when the party scattered out in an attempt to surround them, they made off. They waded in a slough near by, and when passing over a rise of ground beyond, Glispin and Will Estes fired at them with their rifles, just grazing the shoulder and cutting the shirt of one, as they afterwards learned.

This caused the miscreants to hasten their pace, and while those pursuing were crossing the slough and going cautiously up the hill (fearing an ambuscade,) they had made quite an advance. As they were on foot, it was now evident from the direction they were taking that they knew the country, and were making for Doolittle's herd. It was not long before they reached the Hanska slough which they waded, The party in pursuit, who were proceeding in a form of line, came to the slough and finding they could not cross, Glispin and Estes went down the slough and crossed at the house of A. Swingler, who showed them a cattle crossing. The Sheriff sent Severson to show those citizens coming, which way to proceed. Vought went up stream and crossed, and about this time was joined by Dr. Overholt, and coming down to the right of the robbers, fired occasionally to attract others. Dr. Overholt shot with his rifle and hit one of the robber's canes. Glispin and Estes coming up on the left, fired several shots, and the robbers returned the fire, and being at close range, the bullets flew thick about the pursuers, grazing Glispin's horse.

About half past 12 o'clock Will Estes ran out of ammunition and was obliged to come to town, informing those whom he met where to go, and as soon as he arrived here sent telegrams to St. James of movements.

In the pursuit, Glispin, Vought and Overholt saw Doolittle's herd and bore to the right to prevent the robbers from capturing the horses, and crossed the river at J. Doolittle's; some men were ordered to stay there as guard.

FINDING THEMSELVES FOILED

the bandits went to the river opposite Andrew Andersen's house and called to him to bring over his horses, that they were after the robbers. He took the hint however and ran the horses off. The robbers then passed up the river to the next house and crossed at a ford; then passed through Anderson's cornfield to a granary, then seeing teams that Mr. Horace Thompson, President of the First National Bank of St. Paul, had out hunting, they started east toward them, but Mr. Thompson and his son put coarse shot in their guns and faced them, seeing which the robbers turned north down the bluff and crept along in a band in the brush to the bank of the river.

Sheriff Glispin, and others, came down to Andersen's house, and citizens arriving, the Sheriff posted pickets along the bluff on the south side of the river, to watch the robbers. Among these, August Fedder and Wm. Shannon were by the house, Ole Stone on the bluff, and G. W. Green on a point east of the picket line on the north side. At this time J. Dolittle came down and said the guards at his house had gone, and the Sheriff, T. L. Vought and Dr. Overholt returned there to see to it, and the latter was stationed there by the Sheriff.

Meanwhile citizens were arriving on the north side of the river, and some of them saw the robbers go into the brush. About 1 o'clock Capt. W. W. Murphy arrived and having definitely ascertained where the villains were, and also that the citizens were unorganized, all willing but no one deciding what to do, he appeared to take in the situation immediately and at once took command and found every one well pleased to obey. After giving directions concerning the horses, he led forward to the north bank of the river, the stream being about 20 feet wide, and the prairie reaching to the water edge. Here he posted the men at equal distances, each with instructions how to act. The names of the men so posted were Geo. P. Johnston, T. Toren, W. H. Borland, C. Pittis. D. Campbell, Geo. Carpenter, Joe Crandall, H. Juveland, H. H. Winter, Chas. Ash, E. H. Bill, E. A. Loper, J. E. Smith, D. Brayton, J. A. Gieriet, Jack Delling, W. H. H. Witham, Robt. Shannon, W. Bundy, Isaac Bundy, G. Christopherson, and in a few moments these were joined by F. D. Joy, G. W. Yates, H. P. Wadsworth, O. C. Cole and several others.

DIAGRAM OF THE BATTLE FIELD AT MADELIA.

After giving instructions on the north side of the river, Capt. Murphy mounted his horse, and crossed the river on a bridge to the east of where the robbers were. Soon after, he reached the place where

THE BANDITS DESCENDED THE BLUFF

into the brush, when they saw H. Thompson, and gave some necessary instructions there—the Sheriff being absent with T. L Vought at J. Doolittle's. Capt. Murphy after having a hurried consulation with. Ben Rice, put his horse in charge of Alba Crandall, who led several other horses, whom he posted on a slight knoll. Then he stepped to the edge of the bluff and called for volunteers to skirmish the brush, which is in a circular form and contains about 5 acres and is situated in the northeast quarter section 20, township 107, range 31. This brush is willows and plumtrees, interspersed with vines. Ben Rice and Geo. Bradford immediately volunteered, followed by Chas. Pomeroy and James Severson. At this moment T. L. Vought arrived, who immediately dismounted and joined.

Sheriff Glispin then came up and joined the party just as they were starting off. The Capt. gave the men orders to keep in line at an interval of 3 or 4 paces and in case the enemies were found, to rush upon them; to examine their guns carefully, and to shoot low. The line advanced as fast as possible into the brush and passed through to the river, then made a wheel to the left and passed up the river westward, with the right of the line near enough to see the water. After advancing in this direction about ten rods, a shot was fired from a very thick clump of willows, at a distance of fifteen feet from the right of the line. As the shot was fired, the robbers were seen obsecurely in a kneeling position, close together. Glispin returned the fire on the instant with a breech-loading carbine, and dropped to load. As four of the robbers commenced firing as fast as possible, they being armed with Colt's, and Smith and Wesson's six shooters, army size. Capt. Murphy opened fire at this close range with a Colt revolver; Rice discharged his carbine, then fired his pistol; Vought and Pomeroy fired with double-barreled shot guns, and Bradford and Severson with carbine and rifle. Just at this time Captain Murphy received a 44 calibre pistol shot, the ball striking a

BRIAR ROOT PIPE

in his vest pocket, smashing it to pieces, tearing the pocket to shreds, and the ball lodged in the lining of his vest. The blow raised a painful contusion on his side. Bradford also received a slight wound on the wrist, drawing blood. The bandits then retreated a little, firing as they did so, and being discovered by the men posted across the river on the north side, several shots were fired from there. Most of the charges in the skirmish line being exhausted, a slight cessation of firing took place, when the robbers cried out to cease firing, as they were all shot to pieces, the only one able to stand being Bob Younger, he held up his hand in token of surrender. He was immediately ordered to advance, several guns of the skirmishers being held on him till he was relieved of his belt and arms by Capt. Murphy, and assured of protection from further injury. Bob had received one wound in the breast; Cole and Jim Younger were completely riddled—Cole having received eleven and Jim five wounds—they were laying near together. Charley Pitts lay further to the right of the line, dead, having received five wounds, three of which would have caused death.

The robbers had two revolvers a piece, and some of them were ivory handled, nickle-plated, the finest ever seen in this part of the country, and their belts full of bullets.

After their surrender they were taken in charge by Sheriff Glispin, who had them taken to this place in a wagon, followed by the enthusiastic crowds, composed of those engaged in the capture, and those met on the way down, the place where they were taken being about seven miles from here. We are told that it

LOOKED LIKE AN ARMY

coming as they neared town, and when cheers were raised over the victory, the bandits swung their hats, too.

When they arrived here, they were taken to the Flanders House, and their wounds dressed by Drs. Cooley and Overholt.

They were kept under guard at the hotel. During their stay here they were seen by over three thousand persons, and their wounded appearance and pretenses of contrition drew forth a manifest sympathy from some, but this humane conduct of such has been very much exaggerated.

On Saturday morning, Sheriff Glispin, with B. Rice and Captain Murphy as special deputies, started with the wounded bandits for Faribault, arrived in due time and delivered the prisoners to the Sheriff of Rice Co., that being the county in which their crime was committed. The dead robber was taken to St. Paul, by Geo. P. Johnston and G. W, Yates, and delivered to the State authorities for identification. Thus was the career of this band of notorious outlaws brought to an end for the present, with only two of the eight who came into the State escaped, and they wounded. They have raided in thirteen States, but Minnesota proved too much for them, and it is hoped this severe lesson will deter all others of the same stamp from attempting to rob, especially in this State.

A VISIT TO MADELIA.

The first news which reached St. Paul, was "Robbers surrounded in a swamp at Madelia, send long range rifles."

This telegram, however, did not excite so much interest as similar messages had done before, for the people had got weaned of sensational telegrams, but still there were about a score of men willing to go out once more; among these was Chief King and a company of the St. Paul Police, including Brissette. When the train reached Shakopee, however, the news was received of the capture, when King sent back part of his men, the others going to gratify curiosity in seeing the prisoners. The news was expected at nearly every stopping place with the further information that Monty's train would return from St. James and bring the men on to St. Paul.

AT MANKATO,

the excitement was immense. A vast concourse of people—including hundreds of women—had congregated at the depot and cheered the St. Paul train as it drew up. The cars had hardly come to a standstill when a whistle was heard and the discordant clang of a bell which foretold the approach of another train from the west.

A general rush of the assembled throng was at once made to meet the incoming train—Monty's—which was thought to contain the captured bandits. Cheer after cheer rent the air and broke upon the evening's stillness as the train slowly moved up toward the station, but when it was announced that the prisoners were not on board,

DISAPPOINTMENT

took the place of exultation, and many retired with their bitter conviction that the whole thing was a hoax. Twenty minutes for supper, but more than three-fourths of that time had been spent by the writer in interviewing the Mankato party, which had returned from the sanguinary field.

From these he elicited the fact that four of the men were actually in the hands of the Madelia people, and would be sent down in the morning.

ARRIVED AT MADELIA,

the writer hastened to the Flanders House, where he was informed the three prisoners, all wounded, were in bed. Finding the courteous and obliging landlord, he was soon allowed to pass the guard at the foot of the stairs, and ascending, he entered a small chamber, where two men lay in one bed. The first glance told the fact that one of the men was

COLE YOUNGER,

a large, powerful man, with bald head and sandy whiskers and moustache, answering the description, given so many times of this man. He is pretty badly wounded, and at the time was somewhat delirious, so that nothing could be gleaned by questioning him.

His body was full of wounds, mostly caused by buckshot. His worst injuries were about the head, several shot having penetrated the skull and embedded themselves at the base of the brain. It was evident that some of these leaden missiles had lodged among the nerves of the right eye, as that organ was closed and inflamed, and appeared to be forced forward. On entering his head, these shot had broken down the palate arch, and the pain experienced by the prisoner must have been intense. Lying by his side was

JIM YOUNGER,

who is a little shorter, and not nearly of such powerful build. He had quite a number of wounds, the most serious of which was through his mouth, the balls having displaced all of the teeth on one side, and broken the roof of his mouth. His lips and cheeks were terribly swollen, and he could articulate with the greatest difficulty, although he appeared to desire to talk to his visitors.

In another room, about ten yards from the first, lay

BOB YOUNGER,

by far the finest looking man of the whole gang, and apparently the youngest. He is six feet two inches in height, well proportioned, with brawny arms and thick neck. His features are well-defined, well cut lips and expressive mouth; the chin is prominent and rounded; he has a small sandy moustache, and a beard of about two weeks' growth. But the most remarkable feature, after the chin and mouth, is the heavy

PROJECTING CAPACIOUS BROW,

such as phrenologists would give to men of wonderful mathematical ability. This man has two wounds, one an old one, or rather of some days' standing, and supposed to be the result of Wheeler's carbine practice at Northfield, which caused the disarticulation of the right elbow joint. His other wound is from a ball entering the right side, just below the point of the scapula, tracing the sixth rib and coming out near the nipple. This is a mere flesh wound, and not at all dangerous.

At first he seemed rather reluctant to talk much, and when asked his name, he said it was George Huddleston, to which the writer replied, "Oh, I know who you are," when he said, with a cheering smile, "Yes, most people know me in St. Paul. I stayed at the Merchants, and was there when the Red Caps went to Winona to play the Clippers. I afterwards went over to Minneapolis and stopped at the Nicollet, but on my return to St. Paul, I registered at the European."

"But are you not a brother to the two men in the other room?" was asked.

"Yes, we are brothers; we are all brothers, sir," was the reply.

"And they say you are the Youngers. Of course, I know Cole, but I would like to know if you are Jim or Bob?"

"I will tell you in the morning," he said. "I would rather not say anything now. The others will tell you anything you wish to know."

But by chatting familiarly with him, many facts of interest were elicited. He spoke of the Northfield escapade, and said it was the first of the kind he ever was in. When asked about his wound in the right arm, if it was not from the carbine of Wheeler, he stated that he thought it was from the pistol of Bates—he did not see Wheeler. His arm dropped on his leg as described, he said, which led to the belief that he was wounded in the leg.

In speaking of the dead men at Northfield, the writer said that there was some uncertainty whether the big man was Miller or Pitts. The prisoner promptly said, with a smile, "It was not Miller."

He expressed himself freely as to his poor

OPINION OF THE DETECTIVES,

and gave an account of his party's wanderings from Mankato. He said all six crossed the railroad bridge together. They came right through the town on the railroad track. They knew, he said, the other bridge was guarded, for he saw the guards; and then, hastily correcting himself, he said:

"We knew the bridge was watched, and then hastily crossed over on the trestle bridge. We got some melons out of a garden, and on the right of the railroad, a little further down, we got two old hens and one chicken, the only fowls on the place, and then went on to the place where we were disturbed when getting our breakfast ready. We had it all ready to cook when"

WE HEARD THE MEN

"running and shouting up the line and as quickly as we could we got out and crossed the State road (Garden City road.) If we had not left our bridles, the police would not have known we had been there. I had but one arm and I seized my blankets. If I had had two, I should have tried to carry away some of the chicken, for we were dreadfully hungry. After crossing the road we went southeast to the river, ran half a mile up the stream and there laid down all day."

Asked if he did not hear shots fired, he said he did, and saw one of the pursuers within twenty yards of him,

"At night," he continued, "we made across the railroad track again, crossing two or three miles up towards Lake Crystal, and then took a northerly course to the road running due west from Mankato. We then entered the Minnesota timber, where we stayed two nights. Then we made the first of the Linden chain of lakes, I think, and remained in that neighborhood three nights, where we got some chickens. Up to this time we had been"

LIVING ON CORN.

"We were very imprudent, this morning, in going to the house for food, but we were so hungry."

He said the name of the bald-headed man was King, and the one lying dead was Ward. He would tell more, he said, in the morning.

The man has a wonderfully easy manner of speaking. His voice is soft but strong, and marvelously sympathetic and emotional.

THE DEAD MAN

was next interviewed. He was 5 feet 9¾ inches in height, rather slight, with regular features, black straight hair, stubby moustache, black beard of short growth. His hair is not dyed, and is, therefore not a James, for they are light complexioned. Hands rather coarse and covered with black hair. He was shot, with a heavy ball, between the second and third ribs, and one inch to the left of the breast bone. He had also had a buckshot wound in the right arm, five inches from the point of the shoulder and another five inches from the right hip, striking behind.

This man has been identified as Charley Pitts, and recognized by Mr. Bunker as the man who shot him through the arm.

The writer next found the boy who brought in the news to Madelia of the robbers being in the neighborhood.

OSCAR OLESON SUBORN,

is a lad of about seventeen, who said he lives about eight and one-half miles from Madelia, at Linden, Riverdale township. He said that at about seven o'clock in the morning, his father was milking, when two men came past, walking, and said "good morning" and went on. He was coming to the house with milk pails at the time and walked up to the gate, but could not see the faces of the men. But he could see one had a black moustache and the other red whiskers. They went past but he said, "I knew right away"

THEY WERE THE ROBBERS,

and ran out to my father and said, "there goes the robbers." But his father said they were not, and told him to go and attend to his milking. He milked one cow and put the pail inside the gate and ran up the rode which they had gone up. His father halloed after him to come back and to take care of the cows, for if they were the robbers, they would shoot him. He ran on to Mars Ouren's, and asked if he saw the two men pass by. He said he did not see any, when the boy asked the man to go with him to see where the men had gone, but he responded by saying he had no time. He then started off alone, and told Christensen's folks about it, and went on the roof of the house to look around, but could see nobody. He then hurried up to a big hill, and still could not see anybody. When he returned, his father told him that four men had been to get something to eat,

SAYING THEY WERE HUNTERS

and fishers, and asked where they could catch the best fish. The boy ran over to Ouren's again and told them—his father objecting to his going, saying the men would shoot him. His father hitched up the horse in the wagon, but, seeing the boy so anxious to go, said he might take one of the horses and go and tell the people what he had seen, if he went the east road. He at once started for Madelia, riding at the utmost strength of the horse, which once fell and covered him with mud.

"I PICKED UP MYSELF FIRST,"

"and then the horse," he said, "and was soon off again," shouting to everybody to look out, the robbers were about. But no one would believe a word he said. At last he came to the hotel and saw Thomas Vought, who said they might believe him, because he always spoke the truth. He then gave up his horse and returned in a wagon. The people left him to take care of the horses, and they went down to the north branch of the river, by Andrew Andersen's. He heard the shooting, but saw nothing till the men were caught.

DURING THE WHOLE NIGHT

the utmost order prevailed, and no word was spoken of lynching, everybody stating that if such a thing was attempted, they would protect the prisoners with their lives. An inquest was held on the dead man and a verdict found in substance that the man met with his death from the hand of one of the citizens of Madelia while resisting arrest.

THE ROBBERS' LEVEE.

The next morning the Flanders House was literally crammed with eager people, anxious to see the captive bandits, and the street in front was thronged with an equally anxious crowd.

Cole Younger frankly acknowledged their identity, saying that he was Cole, born the 15th of January, 1844. The man lying by his side, he said, was his brother James, and the other, slightly wounded, Robert, their respective ages being 28 and 22 years.

THEY HELD A LEVEE

in their chambers, hundreds of people passing up to see them, old men and youths, aged ladies and young maidens, and a more singular sight is seldom witnessed. Many believe in their contrition. Both brothers spoke in feeling tones of their dead mother and living sister, and this touched the women wonderfully.

Neither would say who the dead man was, excusing themselves by stating it is a point with them never to speak of each other's affairs, only of their own.

The writer mentioned to them that the other two,

THE JAMES BROTHERS

were captured, one dead and the other dying. This seemed to affect them. Cole asked who was dead, the smaller or larger of the two, adding the caution, "mind I don't say they are the James brothers." When the writer said that they had acknowledged who they were, Cole then asked, "Did they say anything of us." When answered in the negative, he replied,

"GOOD BOYS TO THE LAST."

A photograph of the two men killed at Northfield was shown them, and they were told that the shorter was recognized by Kansas City people as Chadwell, and the taller as Miller; also stating that Hazen said the taller was Pitts.

Cole said "they were good likenesses, and cannot but be recognized, but both detectives were wrong." He then added, "Don't misunderstand me; I did not say neither of them was Miller, but there is no Pitts there".

No excitement was feared at Madelia. In fact, there was too much sympathy shown, and every kindness was bestowed upon the captive bandits. Caution was, however, taken to prevent their escape,

ARMED SENTINELS

being placed at the foot of the stairs and about the house.

Friday, in this brave, plucky, generous little town of Madelia, was a day which will long be remembered, not only by the staunch hearts and true of the town, but also by hundreds upon hundreds of visitors, who then for the first time trod its streets, attracted there by the widespread news which suddenly raised the obscure name to a high position upon the roll of fame.

The self-sacrificing heroism of six men made the fame of Colais in the olden time, and the plucky

COURAGE OF SEVEN MEN

has wrung from grudging fortune the renown of Madelia to-day; for throughout the length and breadth of the land, and wherever the pulsations of the electric message-bearer—the nervous system of civilization—was felt, the bosom of generous sentiment swelled with approbation, gratitude, and pride, when the tale of the cool dash and unselfish bravery of those seven Madelians was told. The united voices and hearts of the whole nation swell with gratitude and laudations for Madelia's sturdy heroism.

All day Friday and all the night previous, there was a constant and ever-changing stream of visitors passing through the rooms occupied by Madelia's fated captives. One could but speculate with wonder upon the source of such an inexhuastible human stream.

Not an inconsiderable moiety of the great total of visitors was of the gentler sex, and to one watching with interest the great bandits' matinee and evening receptions, the changing expressions upon the eager, expectant and occasionally indignant countenances of visitors, was of singular interest. A strong, energetic man would enter with knitted brow, and stern, unrelenting features, who would be followed by a timid, half-fearful, half-loathing woman's face. Then there were angry faces, curious faces, bold, proud faces—faces exhibiting every phase of human passion and human temperament—but they had scarcely passed the threshhold of either prison chamber wherein lay the objects of all-absorbing curiosity, when lo! presto! a metamorphose as sudden as it was complete, and as radical as it was rapid, had taken place. Doubt, wonder, and astonishment would grow into

SYMPATHY,

and often admiration. It is safe to say that out of every hundred visitors who looked only for a few seconds upon those daring and notorious men, ninety-nine came away with very different, almost opposite opinions concerning the lawless Younger brothers.

Was it really true that anger, malice, revenge, cruelty, hard, unyielding, implacable hatred ever marred such countenances!—that cold, murderous, steel-like scintillations ever beamed from those eyes? Was it possible that blasphemous execrations and hellish denunciations ever polluted such voices and blistered those pleasant tongues? Was it really true that those three intelligent men—courteous and affable—had plotted and executed some of the most cold-blooded, atrocious diabolisms ever known in modern times? Questions, perhaps, like these, were asked of themselves by hundreds of visitors yesterday, and left unanswered satisfactorily.

COLE YOUNGER

was more demonstrative than either of the rest. He always respected religion, he told one lady. His mother, he said, was a good, praying, Christian woman, and two of his uncles were Methodist ministers.

To another who urged him to pray for himself, for although "the prayers of the righteous availeth much," salvation must necessarily depend upon himself, he said: "I conceive prayer to exist in every action, every thought, and considering the eventful life I have led, I cannot say I have been a praying man. A splendid theme for earnest sermons," he continued, "is that divine mandate, 'Remember thy Creator in the days of thy youth.'"

To another lady he said: "It is not my raising, but from the"

FORCE OF CIRCUMSTANCES,

"I am what I am. Accused of all manner of crimes before I had committed one, I am like the Wandering Jew."

In expressing his gratitude for the kindness manifested by the ladies and the people generally, he said: "It takes a brave man to fight a battle, but a braver man to treat well a fallen foe."

Every lady that entered his room he greeted courteously, and as she was leaving, he would ask her to pray for him and his brother—when James would chime in, "Not for us, never mind us, but pray for our dear sister."

To a group of ladies who shrinkingly looked upon the two wounded men, Cole said: "Ladies, this is a terrible sight." When one asked him in trembling, gentle tones, "Do your wounds pain you?" his reply was, "Wounds do not trouble me, madam; I would as leave die as be a prisoner."

WHEN ASKED ABOUT HEYWOOD,

he said that ninety-nine out of a hundred would have opened the safe. "At least," he added, "I know I would."

Asked why Heywood was shot, he said, "he supposed the man who shot him, whoever he might be, thought Heywood was going to shoot him. The fact that the man was on the counter and turned round, as the papers say, and shot him, is sufficient proof of this. Heywood went to his desk and the man thought chat he was about to take a pistol out of the desk." "That was an unfortunate affair," he continued, "and the man who did it, no doubt regretted it immediately."

BOB YOUNGER,

the youngest brother, is not disposed to talk cant, but answers questions frankly and promptly when directed to his own affairs, but he will not answer a word about any other member of the gang. When asked if he did not think Heywood a brave fellow, he remarked that he thought he acted from fear throughout. He was too much frightened to open the safe, or he could not do it. He (Bob) was was of the opinion that Heywood could not open the safe, and he did not wish to go any further with that job. When asked

WHY HEYWOOD WAS SHOT,

he said it was not on account of revenge, but simply in self-defense, "for what object could there be in such a cold-blooded crime, when the party must be the sufferers. It was a very unfortunate affair for us," he said.

Bob did not hesitate to answer any question proposed to him which concerned himself. He volunteered the statement that he was one of the three who entered the bank, and it was he who tried to keep Manning from firing up the street. Being asked if he was not considered a good shot, he said he had always considered himseif a good marksman, but he thought that he would now have to forego all claim to being a crack-shot, after considering the unusually bad shooting he made in the bush when captured.

To the boy who put the Mankato men upon the track, Cole extended his hand, and said:

"READ YOUR BIBLE,"

"my lad, and follow its precepts. Do not let them lead you astray. For your part in our capture I freely forgive you."

Every opportunity he could get when ladies were present, he would ask them to pray for him, and he would incessantly talk on religious subjects and his previous history, laying the blame of his position to the "force of circumstances," tracing the beginning of his trouble to the "murder of his father by a band of militia thieves."

He said that many of the great crimes for which he and his companions were blamed, he had nothing at all to do with.

There were not a few of the visitors who were of the opinion that Cole Younger was

FOXING IT,

and that he was trying to play off the "pious dodge," awakening commisseration and sympathy from the tender-hearted and religious. The asperity and bitter irony shown when a lady less sympathizing and more matter of-fact than most of his visitors spoke severely of his disgraceful position and degraded life led many to think that Cole is a consumate actor and an arch hypocrite.

When asked why they went to the Northfield bank, and whether it was not more risky than even Mankato banks, he said he told the others at the first that it was

A DANGEROUS UNDERTAKING,

and if they had taken his advice, they would not have gone out to Northfield. There was no means of getting away, for the roads were bad and the woods filled with lakes and sloughs. It would have been better for the band to have gone across the prairie from Mankato, for then they would have had some $30 each.

He was asked if he had tried to shoot any one, when he pointed out the fact that seven of the men were almost within hand's-reach of them, and asked what good would it have done him if all the seven were killed. There were men enough at long range with rifles to shoot him and his party down at their leisure.

While Bob Younger was conversing with the writer, a poor woman came into the room, sobbing, "Don't you know me?" she said, addressing Bob.

"No, madame, I have not that pleasure," said Bob.

"Don't you know me?" reiterated the woman between her sobs.

"Indeed, I cannot recollect you, madame," replied Bob, gently.

"Don't you remember the woman who gave you bread and butter?" she asked.

"Oh yes, certainly; and most thankful were we for it," he replied.

"Oh, forgive me, sir," she sobbed, "indeed, I did not intend to do it."

"I have nothing to forgive," said Bob; "you were very kind to us and we shall not forget it."

"But forgive me, sir," she persisted, "I did not mean to betray you."

"Why, really, madam, we never supposed you did. We did not blame you at all. We are only very grateful for what you did for us."

"But, sir. it was because you were at our house you were caught; but it"

WAS NOT MY FAULT,

"indeed it was not."

Bob, concerned, "I hope you won't trouble about it, madam. It is nothing. We cast the die and lost, and do not blame you in the least. We are only very thankful for what you did."

"But forgive me," persisted the poor woman, "I am so sorry," and she began again to shed tears.

"I have nothing to forgive, only to be grateful for," said Bub, "but if it will make you feel better, I will say I forgive you,"

The poor woman seemed to be greatly relieved and left the room, when Bob turned round to the writer with a concerned and troubled look, and asked the woman's name.

"Mrs. Suborn, the mother of the lad who informed the people of your whereabouts," was the reply.

"I shall never forget that name," said Bob.

The cashier of the First National Bank of Mankato coming in asked Bob if he did not change a bill at his bank. Bob replied promptly that he did—a $50 bill, "But" said he, "you were not in the bank at the time, we were, however, merely giving you a call, only a little matter prevented it, and we unfortunately went to Northfield instead." The cashier asked what their intentions were in Mankato. To which Bob replied that they intended to go through both banks—the City and First National, and he thought that it would have been a much safer job than the Northfield. No doubt the "little circumstance" he alluded to as destroying their plans was the fact of Jesse James being recognized by Robinson, as related elsewhere.

Friday evening at supper time, when the dining hall of the hotel was crowded, at one of the table, there were dark whispers and ominous

THREATS OF LYNCHING,

and some talk, of several hundred people coming up from St. Paul and Northfield to carry out the disgraceful threat. This was sufficient to rouse the precautionary energy of Sheriff Glispin, who at once appointed an armed guard, which filled the entire hotel. The guard and the populace generally were determined to protect their prisoners to the bitter end, if the worst came to the worst, and at half past eight o'clock the hotel was cleared, but on the arrival of the 9 p. m. train, it was found that the rowdies had either missed the train, or had abandoned the scheme, or the whole thing, (which was most probable) was a hoax.

The talk at the supper table arose from a man recently from Mankato, asserting that the scoundrels should be lynched, offering to bet $500 that they would be strung up before morning. It was said that the man was intoxicated, but that was no palliation of his brutish threat.

DISPOSITION OF THE CAPTIVES.

As soon as the news of the capture was received at St. Paul, Captain Macy, secretary to the Governor, telegraphed the executive, then at the Centennial, the fact. The Governor promptly responded, directing Capt. Macy to order the Madelia authorities to bring their prisoners, with the body of the dead bandit to this city. Capt. Macy spent about two hours in telegraphing with the sheriff of the county, who at first strongly opposed the removal, partly on the ground the wounded men were not in a condition to be moved, but principally from a fear that had somehow taken possession of the minds of those taking part in the capture, that their removal to St. Paul would invalidate their claim for the reward offered for their arrest. To this latter objection Capt. Macy answered that the Governor would be responsible for the preservation of all their rights, upon which the Sheriff telegraphed they would be sent down by the morning train, on a sleeper tendered for that purpose, by Supt. Lincoln. Later, however, the sheriff, in consultation with citizens, changed his mind, and determined to send his prisoners on to Faribault, the county seat of Rice county. Accordingly they were placed in the cars at Madelia on Saturday morning, and at every station en route a curious and eager mob awaited the arrival of the train, anxious to get a glimpse of the notorious freebooters. At Mankato, half the city turned out, and arrangements were made at the depot for the crowd to pass through and feast their eyes upon the big show.

At Faribault the crowd was comparatively small, owing, perhaps, to the fact that they were unexpectedly brought on by a freight train, but when it got generally noised about that the infamous desperadoes were lodged in the jail, people of all classes and both sexes thronged the building anxious to gain admittance.

AT ST. PAUL,

Capt. Macy received a telegram from Sheriff Barton, of Rice county, as follows: "I start for Madelia in half an hour. Will bring them by St. Paul."

Saturday morning thereafter, about eleven o'clock crowds began to gather along the bluffs and on the bridge and in any position in which a view of the Sioux City train (on which it was supposed the robbers were being brought to the city) could be obtained. The train was seen crossing the river and immediately the crowd commenced swarming like a hive of bees. As the train approached, and when it came in front of the open space above the upper elevator, the rear platform of the cars appeared to be crowded with people, one man waving a roll of white paper. Then the excitement seemed to culminate. Crowds rushed down the streets in danger of being crushed under the wheels of buggies, wagons and vehicles of all descriptions, which dashed down the streets at a rate which set all ordinances at defiance, and scattered the mud around in a promiscuous manner. At reaching the levee a crowd of fully three thousand people in a terrible state of excitement, were assembled, some climbing up on the still moving train in spite of all efforts of the officers to prevent them, while others ran ahead of the engine and alongside. It soon became evident, however, that the prisoners were not aboard, and a rumor got afloat that they had been taken off the train at Chestnut street and brought to the county jail from thence.

Then there was a scattering among the crowd, and a race was made for the jail, where the moving mass was equally disappointed. Here a large number of persons had already congregated and secured seats around the several entrances of the portico of the Court House, and everywhere where there was a chance of seeing anything.

Here they waited patiently for a while, when some one started a story that the prisoners would be brought through the Fifth street entrance, and a run was made up Cedar street for that point. On arriving there they were assured that no prisoners had been brought into the jail through that entrance, and the idea began to creep through their brains that they had been badly sold. Some, however, could not be persuaded but that they would be smuggled into the building, when the crowd had dispersed, and after waiting for a considerable time longer, reluctantly coming to the conclusion that there was no chance for them to satisfy their curiosity with a sight of the desperadoes, slowly and reluctantly left the ground, and the square surrounding the jail was soon abandoned to its usual and casual passers by and occupants of the several offices.

The dead man, Charley Pitts, was brought on to St. Paul and placed under the care of Dr. Murphy, Surgeon General of the State, for embalming. He was exhibited to an admiring throng of St. Paulites, who being disappointed in not having the big show of real live bandits, were obliged to content themselves with the dead one.

MR. JAMES MCDONOUGH,

chief of police at St. Louis; a member of the police force of that city; and Mr. C. B. Hunn, superintendent of the U. S. express company, arrived in St. Paul on Saturday morning. These gentlemen came for the purpose of establishing the identity of the robbers. They were satisfied those killed at

Northfield, were Bill Chadwell and Clell Miller, immediately recognizing their photographs.

Chief McDonough is a straight, fleshy gentleman, with a military bearing, a keen eye, and the appearance of a man possessed of the executive ability requisite to control and conduct so great a force of men, (over five hundred,) as compose the splendid police force of the city of St. Louis. He had obtained from Hobbs Kerry, one of the gang engaged in the bold raid on the train at Otterville, Mo., July 7th, detailed descriptions of the other members of the gang, and early yesterday morning he visited the capitol to view the body lying there. As soon as he looked upon it he recognized it as Charley Pitts, whose real name is George Wells. Every mark was found as detailed by the captured robber, and the chief was evidently pleased to find that he had succeeded in getting so much truth out of one of the members of a gang whose honor is pledged not to "peach" on their comrades. One of the most noticeable peculiarities of Pitts, who is a man of most powerful build, is his extremely short, thick feet. They require but number six boots, and look inadequate to support the ponderous form above. His hands, which are also small and fat, were roughened by work, and covered with black hair, exactly as Kerry had said. From Mr. McDonough, it was learned that Pitts is one of the men who are summoned when "dirty work" is on hand. His home is in Texas, and he is known as one of the boldest and most successful horse thieves in the country. His knowledge of horses is so great, that the care of the stock of the gang is always confided to him.

DETECTIVES' TRIP TO FARIBAULT.

Having decided the identity of Pitts, the officers returned to the Merchants' Hotel, and it was arranged that a special train should be procured to transport them, in company with several officials of this city, and a few well known citizens, to Faribault to interview his

BROTHERS IN CRIME.

The train was ready at about 1:30, Superintendent Lincoln having, at very short notice, provided an engine and an elegant passenger coach. Among the few that took passage in the train, were Chief McDonough, Mr. Russell, and Superintendent Hunn, of the United States Express Company, all of St. Louis; Mayor Maxfield, Chief King, Captain Webber, Captain Macs, Dr. Murphy, Col. John L. Merriam and his sons, W, R. Merriam, cashier of the Merchant's National Bank, and master John L., Jr., who was with his father at the time of the Gad's Hill robbery three years ago; Superintendent Lincoln (who was also a victim of the same raid), Col. Hewitt, R. C. Munger, H. H. Spencer, of West Wisconsin railroad; Mayor Ames, of Northfield, and

A LARGE NUMBER OF LADIES,

who desired to look upon the desperate fellows, but who evinced no more curiosity than their male comrades.

The run to Faribault was accomplished at about 4 o'clock. During the ride a most open discussion of the situation of the affair took place, and there was no concealment of the disappointment felt of any of the bandits being taken alive, and the desire was freely expressed that the three

BLOODY BANDITS

should not be permitted to take advantage of the clemency which the laws of Minnesota afford to a self-convicted murderer.

The news that a special train was *en route* had been kept so quiet, that on arriving at Faribault, no persons were at the depot except the officers of the road and Mr. Case, with several omnibuses. It had been arranged that only a select few should visit the jail with the detectives, and but eight persons, including the writer were admitted, the remainder of the party separating and seeking a lunch before they interviewed the outlaws.

During the entire day there had been a constant stream of visitors from the adjacent country, who came in all sorts of conveyances, the citizens of Faribault giving way to them and awaiting a quieter time to call on their distinguished guests.

The jail was surrounded by men and women when the chosen delegation arrived, but by an arrangement with Sheriff Barton, the crowd was restrained, and the St. Louis gentlemen, Mayor Maxfield, Chief King, Captain Macy, Dr. Murphy, Messrs. Lincoln and Merriam, and representatives of the St. Paul dailies were admitted.

On entering, Bob Younger was found sitting near the corner of the cage, quietly smoking a cigar with a newspaper on his lap. Cole was lying on a pallet at the end of the twenty foot jail outside the cage, with a cigar in his mouth and a daily paper before him. The lazy bandit was being fanned by a boy, and seemed wonderfully comfortable. The third man was lying on a cot just inside the bars, and was evidently suffering severely from the wound in his mouth.

Cole Younger was found communicative as usual. Chief King, showed him pictures of the two James boys, taken eight years since, and he immediately knew them, but said nobody would recognize them from those pictures now. On looking at his own picture he acknowledged it as one of the best he ever had taken, but when he looked at that of Charley Pitts, he said he knew no man of that name. Chief King said: "But you know this man as Wells," when Cole responded, "There are Wellses in every part of the country."

At this time Mr. Ames, of Faribault, came up and asked what part he took in the affair at Northfield. He declined to tell. Mr. A. then said he thought he rode a white faced horse, and was the man that shot the Swede. Cole denied this. Ames said that man was observed as the best horseman of the crowd. Younger then said one man was as good a rider as another. He was raised on a saddle, his father having been a herder and stock man, and besides, he had served several years in the cavalry. The gentlemen then spoke of the killing of Heywood as a cowardly act. Cole said it was the result of impulse, as they did not intend to kill anybody. Their plan was to accomplish their ends by dash, and boldness, and to do the robbing while men were frightened. This was denied by the Northfield man, who claimed that they tried hard to kill Manning. Cole then said that they did not try to kill him, using his name as if he knew all about it, but fired all around him. Mr. Ames said that could not be true, as shots were found in the railing of the stairs behind which Manning stood. Younger denied this, and said they desired to kill no man, as it would be of no use to them. Ames then said he believed they had killed a hundred men, when Cole said he had no time to talk with such a man, he had been captured by brave men, and was being treated better than he deserved, that he did not fear death, but hoped to be prepared for a better world. He said he was tired and needed rest. At this, an impulsive gentleman standing by said he wished he would soon take his long rest. Cole seemed offended at this, and said it was "of no" use to talk to illiterate people, they could not

"APPRECIATE A SUBLIME LIFE!"

Cole said he did not ride his fine horse up here, but bought the one he rode of French, of St. Peter. When told by a visitor that they did bad shooting, he said if they would prop him up at the side of the road he would plug his hat with his left hand at ten rods every time. He said he was the man that took the pistols from the dead man at Northfield; and said he took his handkerchief out of his belt as he took it off. He declined to tell the name of the dead man, as it was understood none should tell about another dead or alive.

Col Merriam sat by the side of Cole, and said, "Younger, I am not certain, but I think I have seen you before." "Where was this?" said Cole. The Colonel said it was at Gad's Hill three years ago when the raid was made on the train. This, Cole denied, and said that at that time he was in St. Clair county, in Southwestern Missouri, where his uncle, Judge Younger resides. He said he would refer to his uncle, who is a judge, and was a member of the legislature, and also to a minister there. He further said that on the day of that raid he and his brother Robert were there, and that he preached in the afternoon, commencing at four o'clock.

Col. Merriam feels sure that Cole was there, judging from his figure, his hair, and particularly by his voice. Mr. Lincoln is also certain that he was one of the men on the train at that time, although he wore a cloth with eye holes over his face. Master Merriam, who was also on the train, is not certain, but thinks he has seen the villain.

Bob Younger was asked if he was in the Gad's hill raid, but denied it, saying he was in Louisiana at that time, thus contradicting Cole. Bob says he is a novice, and has only been in a few scrapes.

While some of the visitors were talking with the boys, Mr. McDonough, his aid, and Dr. Murphy, were examining the prisoners for marks of identification, and no trouble was experienced in placing Cole and Bob Younger, but the identity of the one that claimed to be Jim, was doubted by the detectives, as James was badly wounded in the hip on the 7th of July last, and they thought he could not possibly be able to stand a campaign like this at present. They were of the opinion that he was Cal. Carter, a Texas desperado, and one that has seldom worked with a gang until lately.

Every point of identification as given by Hobbs Kerry, was discovered on the Younger boys, even to the ragged wound on Bob's hand, where the thumb had been torn off and badly attended to.

Dr. Murphy said none were dangerously injured, and "are sure to get well unless he doctors them." He made a careful examination and said they had only flesh wounds, and that the men could be about in a few days. None of the prisoners were shackled, and as the writer came out (he being the last one of the visitors), Cole Younger got up from his bed and walked across the jail as lively as he.

When the robbers were captured their clothes and boots were found in a bad state. The three living robbers had each five dollars in their pockets, and the dead one had one dollar and a half. According to the statement of

Bob Younger, all of the money, watches and jewelry they had was given to the two robbers that escaped, as they felt that their chances of getting away were much the best.

IMPRISONMENT AND TRIAL.

Great fears were entertained that the Rice county jail at Faribault, would not be of sufficient strength to hold the three famous bandit brothers, of whose great desperation and accomplishment in the art of prison breaking, the most wonderful and exaggerated stories were circulated throughout the State. Sheriff Ara Barton, however, did not hesitate to accept his distinguished boarders, and probably a thought of their escape from him never entered his mind. He had the bandits in his care, and he proceeded in the most systematic manner to provide for their remaining with him. No effort was made to strengthen the jail, but a series of guards was arranged so that the inside and outside were both constantly under the eye of watchful guards. The only fears entertained by those having the robbers in charge, were that there might be efforts made from the outside, either by a mob who would seek to lynch the brigands, or by their own friends, who would undertake to liberate them. For both cases, Sheriff Barton was prepared.

A COMPANY OF MINUTE MEN

was formed by citizens of the city, and the bell of an adjacent engine house was connected with the guard room of the jail by a wire. In case of any attack, these fifty men, armed with repeating rifles, were to rendezvous at a certain point from whence, under their captain, they would proceed in order to the jail. Another wise precaution taken by the Sheriff was in the locking of the doors of the jail, which are about 18 inches apart. He kept the key of the inner one himself, while the guard inside retained that of the outside door. At a private signal, the guard would reach through and unlock the outer one, when the Sheriff would find use for his key on the inner one. Several guards kept constant watch night and day around the jail, and at its entrance, a cannon loaded with a blank cartridge stood, ready to give a general alarm. As an instance of how perfect the arrangements were, it may be stated that on one occasion when the fire bell sounded, in less than three minutes the jail was surrounded by men, some carrying guns, some bludgeons, and some farm tools. Any party foolish enough to have undertaken the rescue of those

THREE BANDITS,

would have been made short work of, while a mob, with the intention of disposing of them unlawfully, would have been met with a determined opposition, for the entire male population of Faribault were determined to support the Sheriff, and bring the murderers to trial.

Notice of the arrangements about the prison were published, and all people were warned from approaching the jail in the night time, but one man, belonging to the police force of the city, thought he was so well known to the guards that he could safely visit them, and one evening he walked toward the prison. One of the guards challenged him, but instead of replying, he raised his hand to his coat, to make his silver star visible, and at the same moment, the guard mistaking the movement and supposing that the man was reaching to his breast pocket for a pistol, fired, inflicting a wound that proved fatal soon afterwards. Thus was another tragedy added to the list, and the horror of the affair was intensified.

Thus for a month everything moved quietly along about Governor Barton's hotel, and he remained unmoved by the hundreds of threats and propositions he received. He is a brave man made of stern stuff, and when a proposition was made to him to remain neutral while a posse that was being organized, opened the jail and took the bandits out to

THE NEAREST TREE,

he coolly told their messenger, who was a prominent man in the State, and a personal friend of his, "that if they came, no matter who they were, they would be shot down like dogs." This remark was repeated to the party who proposed the lynching, by Mayor Nutting, and people began to think it was best to abandon the project of anticipating the law, while the Younger boys remained in such hands. However, there is no doubt but that a summary disposal of these bloody cut-throats would have been widely endorsed by the best men of the State, as the feeling existed that no villians ever merited death more than they, while under the law of Minnesota, they could escape with a life sentence, with the possibilities of escape or pardon.

INSIDE THE JAIL.

Under the best of medical care the Younger boys rapidly recovered from their wounds, and in less than two weeks, Cole and Jim were up and about, looking as well as ever, except that Cole had suffered a partial paralysis of the right eye, which had a wild, rolling look, and which was forced forward to an unpleasant prominence, caused by the buckshot that still remained in his head, and which he refused to allow the Doctors to remove, as he said they did not incommode him.

Jim's wounds on the outside of his face healed finely, and he proved to be a mild, pleasant and inoffensive fellow, appearing entirely incapable of such bloody work as that in which he had taken part, and strengthening the belief in the story that he had been prevailed upon contrary to his inclination. All of his back teeth had been carried away by the shot, and the roof of his mouth shattered, causing him much inconvenience in talking and eating, but his appetite was good, and he managed to do full justice to the liberal rations his hospitable host provided.

Bob enjoyed perfect general health, but the wound through the elbow of his right arm promised to incapacitate him, as it was rigidly stiff. The surgeons decided on a severe operation, and Bob carelessly submitted while the joint was broken and re-set. Then a hinge-like holder was placed around the wounded limb, and by slightly moving the joint each day, the arm was saved, and he is now able to make himself useful at light work in the State prison.

The bandits occupied the jail with a number of other prisoners, and were kept inside a series of strong iron bars that divided the cells from the corridor. Manacles were kept upon their legs, and the eye of a guard was never off them. They occupied their time in reading and writing, and Cole devoted himself almost constantly to reading the Bible, taking occasional instruction from the revised statutes of the State, relating the punishment of murderers. All were humble and patient, except that the independent Bob, when the subject of hanging was under discussion, would boldly claim that "they could not hang him for what he never did."

IN COURT.

On the 7th day of November, the district court of Rice county convened in Faribault. Judge Sam'l Lord presiding. The first duty of the sheriff, was to present the names of twenty-two grand jurors, which he did on the 8th inst.

The Younger brothers had engaged Mr. Thomas Rutledge, of Madelia, as their counsel, and had subsequently associated with him, Messrs. Batchelder and Buckham, of Faribault, two of the most eminent lawyers of the State. The prosecution was in the hands of George N. Baxter, Esq., the county attorney of Rice county, and he had woven a strong chain of evidence about the prisoners, having traced them and their comrades through all their journeying from the time they entered the State until the raid was made.

The prisoners' counsel had long interviews with their clients, and it was generally understood that, in case they were indicted for murder in the first degree, they would plead "not guilty." This was taking a risk, as in case they were found guilty, the death penalty could be inflicted at the option of the jury, and it would have been difficult to find a jury but that would have quickly pronounced a doom so much in accordance with public sentiment.

The county attorney, Mr. Baxter, drew and presented four indictments for the consideration of the grand jury, one charging them collectively with being accessory to the murder of Heywood, a second, charging them with attacking Bunker with intent to do great bodily injury; a third, charging them with robbing the bank at Northfield; and a fourth, charging Cole with the murder of the Swede, and his brothers as accessories.

When Cole Younger read the last named indictment, he appeared greatly affected, and said that he had not expected such a bill, as he did not kill the Swede. He said it had probably been done by accident, as none of them shot to kill. From the time the indictments were read by Cole, he became low-spirited, and studied the statutes and consulted with his lawyers more than before. Bob kept up, and declared that he would not plead guilty in any case.

THE GRAND JURY

that had been summoned included twenty two of the best men in the county, but the prisoner's counsel reduced it to seventeen, by challenging a number who had too freely expressed their ideas in regard to the affair. There is no doubt but that by continuing the same line of questioning the grand jury could have all been found wanting, but it was not the intention of the defense to delay the trial by reducing the number below the legal minimum, but simply to refer the bills to as few men as possible, feeling that the chance of their finding all of the indictments could be materially lessened.

It took the jury but a very short time after they commenced their work to find four true bills against the prisoners, and the evidence given by the witnesses that testified before them, was but a recapitulation of what they were entirely familiar with. In the case of the Swede, whom Cole Younger was charged with killing, evidence was given by a man and a woman, both of whom testified that they saw Cole shoot him coolly and deliberately.

IN THE COURT ROOM.

On the day after the court convened, the sister and an aunt of the Younger boys arrived in Faribault. The sister, Miss Henrietta Younger, is a very pretty, prepossessing young lady of about seventeen years, and she conducted herself so as to win the esteem of all who met her. Mrs. Fanny Twyman, their aunt, is the wife of a highly respectable physician practicing in Missouri, and appears to be a lady of the highest moral character. These ladies passed the greater portion of their time sitting with their relatives, behind the iron bars, reading, talking and sewing. On Thursday, the 9th of November, the grand jury signified that they had completed their labors as far as the cases of the Younger boys were concerned, and the sheriff was instructed to bring the prisoners to hear the indictments read.

This summons had been expected, and the boys were ready, dressed neatly, and looking wonderfully well after their unaccustomed confinement that had continued for more than a month. They quietly stood up in a row ready to be shackled together. Cole in the middle, Bob at the right, and Jim at the left. The shackles were placed on their feet; Bob being secured by one foot to Cole, and Jim by the other. When the handcuffs were placed on Cole, he remarked, that it was the first time he had ever worn them. The prisoners showed signs of nervousness, evidently fearing that the crowd outside would think it best to dispose of them without due process of law. However, nothing occurred except some almost inaudible mutterings among the spectators, but which were quickly quieted by right-minded citizens. Slowly the procession passed to the temple of justice, the prisoners seeing the sun and breathing the pure air for the first time in thirty days. In advance of them was an armed guard, led by the captain of the minute men, then came the sheriff by the side of his prisoners, the chief of police of Faribault, and his lieutenant, and finally another squad of minute men with their needle guns. On reaching the court-house, the guards broke to the right and left, and allowed none to enter except those known to their captain.

The cortege passed to the court room by a rear stairway, and when the prisoners arrived in front of the Judge, the court-room was thoroughly filled with people, all gazing with the greatest curiosity on the three

BLOODY BROTHERS.

The shackles having been removed from the arms and legs of the prisoners, they were ordered to stand up while the indictment charging them with killing Heywood, was read to them by the county attorney. As their names were read, the Judge asked them if they were indicted by their true names, to which all responded in the affirmative. During the reading, Cole Younger never moved his sharp eye from the face of the attorney, in fact, his gaze was so intense, that Mr. Baxter appeared to feel it, and to be made somewhat nervous thereby. Bob did not appear to take great interest in the matter, and he gazed coolly about on the crowd.

The sister and aunt of the boys were by their sides during this scene, and they walked with them as they returned to the jail under the same guard that escorted them forth. Until the following Saturday had been taken by the prisoners' counsel to plead to the indictment, and during the interval of three days the subject of how to plead was discussed for many hours. Bob was as independent as ever, declared he would not plead guilty, but the persuasions of sister and aunt finally prevailed, and when taken into court on Saturday in the same manner as before, each responded

"GUILTY,"

when the question was asked by the clerk. Judge Lord then, without preface or remark, sentenced each to be confined in the State Prison, at Stillwater, at hard labor, for the term of his natural Life. After the dread words had been uttered, the sister broke down and fell sobbing and moaning on the breast of her brother Cole.

Thus these bloody bandits escaped the gallows where their many crimes should have been expiated, and in a few days from the time they were sentenced, they were on their way to Stillwater, under a strong guard, but no attempt was made to molest them, although large crowds were collected at each station on the railroads by which they traveled. Sheriff Barton knew well the citizens of his State, and he had no fear that he would be interfered with while discharging his duty. The bandits were accompanied to their final home in this world by their faithful relatives, who left them within the prison walls, taking away as mementoes the clothes which the wicked men had worn. The robbers were immediately set at work painting pails, a labor which called for no dangerous tools to prosecute, and a special guard was set upon the renowned villains, as it is not intended that they shall escape to again terrify the world by their wicked deeds.

JOSEPH LEE HEYWOOD.

BIOGRAPHICAL

JOSEPH LEE HEYWOOD,

the brave victim of the desperate raid, was born at Fitzwilliam, N. H., August 12th, 1837. He left home when about twenty years of age, and passed the better part of a year in Concord, Mass., and then changed his residence to Fitchburg, remaining there not far from a year. At the age of twenty-three, or in 1860, he came as far west as New Baltimore, Mich., and for some twelve months was occupied as clerk and book-keeper in a drug store. Moline, Illinois, then became his home for a short time, but the war of the rebellion raging, he went to Chicago and enlisted for three years in the 127th Illinois regiment. This was in 1862. Soon after he was ordered to the front and saw not a little of hard service on the march, and on the field of battle. He was present at the unsuccessful attack on Vicksburg, and also at the capture of Arkansas Post. Not long after, his health giving way through exposure and over exertion, he was sent first to the hospital, and then sent, more dead than alive, to his friends in Illinois. A few months later, recovering his health sufficiently to do light service, he was detailed as druggist in a dispensary at Nashville, where he remained until the close of the war, and was discharged in May, 1865. The next year was spent, for the most part, with friends in Illinois, and then we find him, in the summer of 1866, in Minnesota, and in Faribault, and the year after in Minneapolis, in a drug store again. In the fall of 1867, he removed to Northfield to keep books in the lumber yard, for S. P. Stewart. Four years since he accepted the position in the bank which he held till all earthly occupations came to a sudden and untimely end.

He was a man whose integrity and honor were never impeached, a good citizen and neighbor, a friend to be sought, and a loving and loved husband and father.

THE CAPTORS

The following sketches of the intrepid captors who risked their lives in the bush to attack the desperate outlaws, was supplied by W. H. H. Johnston, Esq. for the *Pioneer-Press*, from which it is copied:

SHERIFF JAMES GLISPIN

is an American, of Irish parentage, having a mother, sisters and brothers residing in Watonwan county. He is probably twenty-five or twenty-eight years of age, five feet six inches in height, rather light built, fair complexion, short dark brown hair, and, although in somewhat poor health last year, is one of the quickest and most wiry young men in the county. Possessing not only great physical strength and endurance, whereby I have seen him completely overcome, in several serious disturbances, larger men, boasting of their power and daring, but he has great magnetic and persuasive influence, and I have seen peace restored by his exceedingly quiet presence and determined glance, whereas only a few moments previously it looked threatening and dangerous. No tenderer or kinder-hearted man exists, unless duty compels otherwise. I know in doing business with him as an attorney and the evidence of the other lawyers will be the same, that in every respect he is honorable, fair, and impartial in the discharge of his duty, as well as a perfect gentleman. I always considered him a remarkable young man, all wire and grit. Four winters ago he was in Hon. B. Yates' store as a polite and obliging clerk. The next winter he went to work in a woolen mill at Minneapolis. He was in poor health; came to his home and was nominated on the Democratic ticket as a liberal, against the ex-sheriff, one of the most popular Republicans in the county, and Glispin carried by several hundred in a Republican stronghold. He served faithfully and well two years, and was re-nominated and re-elected again by a large majority, and is on the close of his second term, and I don't see any reason why he should not be a third-termer.

CAPT. WILLIAM W. MURPHY,

was born in Westmorland county, Pennsylvania, and is now about thirty-nine years of age. Went to California in 1854, and after spending several years on the Pacific coast, returned to Pennsylvania in 1861, and entered the service as Second Lieutenant, 14th Pennsylvania Cavalry, September, 1862; soon thereafter promoted to a Captaincy in same regiment for gallantry on the field of Piedmont, under Gen. Davis Hurter. During his term of service he received two sabre and three gun-shot wounds, was mustered out of service with his regiment, September, 1865. The following spring he came to Minnesota and settled at Madelia, Watonwan county. He was elected by the Republicans in 1872, as a member of the Legislature from Watonwan. He is well educated and an intelligent man, especially in the science of agriculture to which he gives great attention and is quite successful. He is noted as being a man of great personal daring and courage.

COL. THOMAS L. VOUGHT,

is a man of forty-five or forty-eight years of age; large, well built man, of fine, imposing personal appearance, and if he looks cross at any one, especially a robber, it would indicate that he meant "business." In fact he is noted as being extremely kind hearted and pleasant in his way and manner, but of great reserve force and determination when necessity requires. Years ago he fought the Indians in that county and weathered many bitter storms, long distances, night and days alone as stage owner and driver and United States mail carrier. He is now well known as the affable owner and host of Flanders Hotel, and has a large local and transient patronage.

GEORGE BRADFORD,

is a young man about twenty-five years of age, son of Morris Bradford, many years a county officer and old resident. He is a partner of J. N. Cheney, merchant, a quiet, handsome gentleman, of splendid business qualifications, of high integrity, regular and attentive to duty, and is highly respected by the community; he is well educated, and formerly was a school teacher in the county. He is very firm and unyielding when pushed.

BENJAMIN M. RICE

resides in St. James, is a young man, son of Hon. W. D. Rice, ex-Senator representing that county and district several terms in both branches of the legislature at St. Paul. Young Mr. Rice was engrossing clerk in the senate some years ago. He was born in the extreme south, and a resident there for several years, and possesses in a remarkable degree the fiery ardor, daring and impetuous power, characteristic of many southern men—even bordering on recklessness. No more lithe, wiry, or difficult man to encounter than he if crossed. He is very familiar with the use of revolvers and weapons, and the equal in accuracy to any one of the robbers. He is a shrewd and successful business man, warm hearted and a thorough gentleman in his manner and address.

JAMES SEVERSON,

is a young Norwegian, about eighteen or nineteen years of age, who came from Iowa to be a clerk two years ago in the large store of G. B. Yates. The jolliest and most popular young man, with everybody, especially his customers. He speaks several languages well. To his wit and gond nature everybody will bear witness, especially the ladies; he is a good salesman, industrious, correct, and to be depended upon; he is short, stout, and a little "daredevil" if any trouble is on hand.

CHARLES POMEROY

is the second son of C. M. Pomeroy, justice of the peace, and who is one of the oldest and most respected residents of the county. The young man is short, compact, powerfully built, and is strong, very quiet and unobtrusive, yet immovable and tenacious when danger threatens; he is a hardworking, industrious farmer boy, and anything that needs coolness, courage and determination to make successful, he would be chosen for it.

OSCAR OLESON SUBORN.

AS HE APPEARED WHEN CARRYING THE NEWS.

OSCAR OLESON SUBORN,

is American born, of Scandinavian parents, and bears a fine reputation for truthfulness and industry. We insert two cuts of this lad, one representing him as he appeared when he carried the news of the robbers presence to Madelia and the other one showing him as he appears when in his best clothes.

THE YOUNGER FAMILY.

[The principal points in the following sketch were furnished by the Younger boys and must be received as in a degree partial.—ED.]

Henry W. Younger, the head of this branch of the Younger family was a native of Kentucky, but early in life he removed to Jackson county, Missouri, in company with his father's family. The family were thoroughly respectable, of more than ordinary intelligence, and comfortably provided with wealth. H. W. Younger proved to be a young man of superior ability, acquiring an excellent education, and occupying a prominent position in the political world. Ho served in the Missouri Legislature, and also as county judge in Jackson county. Col. Younger was married in 1830, and lived in Jackson county until 1858, during which time fourteen children, eight girls and six boys, were born to them.

In 1858 the family moved to a larger farm near Harrisonville, Cass county, where his operations in farming, stock dealing and general trade became extensive, and his wealth rapidly increased. By his decided, and boldly maintained political convictions, he made many enemies—especially during the trouble which occurred between the people of his state and those of Kansas in regard to the admission of the latter as a slave state.

When the civil war broke out in 1861, Younger espoused the Union cause, and on account of his wealth and prominence was made the especial object of the lawless depredations of the "Jayhawkers" of Kansas under Lane, Jemison and others. His property was destroyed, his stock stolen, and he with his family was obliged to flee for their lives.

Early in September 1862 as Col. Younger was driving into Harrisonville, with a large amount of money about him he was robbed and murdered in his buggy. Even after having disposed of the father, his enemies were not satisfied, and their aggressions were directed against the inoffensive widow and her family of young children. They were forced to burn and abandon their own home, and the poor woman found no peace until finally she died in Clay county, Missouri.

THE CHILDREN.

The oldest son Richard had died in 1860 at the early age of 23, after having acquired a liberal education, and became an esteemed member of the Masonic order.

Of the eight sisters six grew up, four being well married, one of the others dying within a few years, and another still living in maidenhood, being the one spoken of herein.

The sons that lived to suffer from the aggressions of the enemies of their father were Thomas Coleman, James Henry, John and Robert Ewing, three of whom are now in the hands of the law officers of Minnesota, and incarcerated in the prison at Stillwater.

No apology would be accepted by the public for the course which these men have pursued since the death of their parents, and no apology will be offered.

"To err is human; to forgive, divine." Forgiveness was not found in these men. Revenge was the impulse that actuated them, and now they accept all mankind as foes. With their education and activity they might doubtless have become esteemed members of other communities, but they preferred to allow their resentment to lead them until they became outlaws and branded criminals. They have stated that they have deliberately chosen their profession, and are prepared to abide by the consequences. The judgment of the world is fixed, let a higher power render the verdict.

COLE YOUNGER.

THOMAS COLEMAN YOUNGER.

This man whose name has become a terror throughout the entire west, was born January 15th, 1844, in Jackson county, Missouri. He was a bright, active lad, and somewhat wild. His education is not such as he might have acquired if he had availed himself of the advantages afforded him in his early youth. He was always full of daring, and was reckoned a keen young chap. He appears to have provoked the hatred of certain officers of the militia under Neugent at the early age of seventeen, and their persecutions, whether just or unjust, caused him to desert his home, even his plan of attending school at a distant place being interfered with.

Early in 1862 Cole joined the famous Quantrell band of guerillas, with whom he remained until late in 1864, when he enlisted in the Confederate army. He became a captain, and remained in the service until the war ended, when he went to Mexico and California, where he stayed until 1866.

Cole now resolved to settle down and redeem the family farm, which had been sadly neglected. His enemies, however, would not permit him to work in peace, and he together with his brothers James and John were forced to go to Texas, where they intended to make a new home for their mother, but she died in 1870, before their plans were completed.

In March, 1875, a preamble and resolution was introduced into the Missouri house of representatives, relating the crimes charged against the Younger brothers, and granting them full amnesty and pardon. It was, however, defeated by a small majority.

Cole Younger possesses talents of no ordinary degree, and his claim that he could never live a reputable life is absurd, as he could have established himself in a distant community or in a foreign land and prospered, if he had so desired. This is proved in the case of his brother James, who, when the Northfield raid was planned, was living and prospering in California, where he had accumulated quite a sum of money and was in a fair way of becoming well off. Money was needed for the enterprise, and after frequent solicitation he was induced to return to his old life and embark his savings in the speculation that has proved so terribly disastrous, and has consigned him to a living tomb.

Cole appears to have early cultivated a taste for the wildest of adventures, and with a ferocity and cruelly almost fiendish, the taking of human life, when it interfered with his plans appears to have been no more to him than the use of hard words among ordinary men. During his connection with the Quantrell gang he was the boldest and bloodiest of the outlaws, and was guilty of many terrible deeds when his passions got the better of his judgment, while at other times he would treat his defeated antagonists with a magnanimity which showed that there was really a heart hidden away somewhere about him. At times he would spare none of his enemies, shooting them down like dogs, even when wounded and unable to defend themselves, and at other times he would himself nurse and comfort his most hated foe.

His statement that he NEVER KILLED A MAN except in legitimate conflict, is of course absurd, and none will believe that a man who has had so desperate an experience as Cole Younger can place any high value upon human life. At horse races, in gambling hells, on the prairies, in railroad trains, and in quiet valleys, he has pursued his nefarious profession, and satisfied his revenge or gained money by force of arms, intimidating and killing those who came in his way.

It is told that at a certain horse race he had wagered money on his horse, but one of the crowd, all of whom were enemies of Cole, by a cowardly trick caused his horse to lose. He forbade the stake-holder to deliver the money to his opponent, and when he insisted upon doing so Cole drew two large pistols and as he dashed away he discharged them into the crowd killing three men, and escaping unharmed.

The exploits of Quantrell and his men have been so often published that it is not necessary to rehearse them at this time, but in nearly all of the most desperate and bloody encounters of the desperate gang Cole Younger played a prominent part. He was appointed to lead the most dangerous expeditions, and his success was such that it appeared as if the DEVIL HIMSELF WERE AT HIS ELBOW.

One of the most sad and cruel murders that Younger was forced to commit, was when, after a visit to his grandmother, he was met on the threshold by his cousin, Captain Charles Younger, who belonged to the militia of the state. The cousins shook hands, after which Captain Younger informed his relative that he was his prisoner. Instantly Cole drew his revolver, and placing it in front of his cousin's face fired, killing him instantly. Although the vicinity was filled with militiamen the guerilla made good his escape with his usual luck.

WHOLESALE KILLING.

It is related that at one time Quantrell's company, after an encounter with a party of jayhawkers, found fifteen prisoners on their hands. As was the custom, arrangements were speedily made to put them to death. Among the arms captured was an Enfield rifle, and as none of the guerillas had ever seen one before, it was decided to test its merits, as they had heard that its force was terrible. The poor prisoners were placed in a row one behind the other, and Cole Younger, claiming that the weapon ought to kill ten men at a shot, deliberately fired at fifteen paces. The rifle disappointed the bloody executioner, as it killed but the first three men. Seven shots were fired by the cruel marksman before the fifteen were disposed of.

AS A FOOT-PAD AND ROBBER

Cole Younger is charged with having been connected with a great number of wild adventures where stages, railroad trains, banks and stores have been robbed, and his connection with them is not doubted by many, although he has proved by respectable parties that he had nothing to do with some of them.

A series of desperate crimes commenced to be committed as early as 1868, and it was evident that a regularly organized band existed. It was, and is, believed that the Younger brothers and the James brothers were the leading spirits of the organization, and that it consisted of desperate characters living in all parts of the western states as far south as Texas and north through the territories. In 1868 a bank was robbed in Russellville, Ky., and a good haul was made. In the same year the bank at Gallaten, Mo., was attacked, and the cashier, J. W. Sheets, was killed.

In August, 1873, the safe belonging to Wells, Fargo & Co's express company was taken from a stage in Nevada territory, by four masked brigands, and broken open and robbed of about $12,000 in gold and greenbacks, while the driver and passengers were prevented from interfering by cocked guns held at their heads.

In January, 1874, a stage en route for the Arkansas Hot Springs, was stopped at Gain's place by five men wearing army overcoats, and all of the passengers were forced to give up all of their money and valuables. There were a number of gold watches taken, the robbers declining to receive any silver ones, and the sums of money received ranged from $5 to $650. The robbers asked if any of the passengers had been in the Confederate army, and when one responded in the affirmative, his property was returned to him, with the remark that they only robbed Northern men, who had driven them into outlawry. Another man who was entirely crippled by rheumatism was not interfered with and was not robbed.

In February, 1874, the First National Bank of Quincy, Illinois, was robbed of over $500,000 in money and bonds, but as the work was done in the night, it is thought that the Younger gang was not concerned in it, as they have never been known as burglars, but bold, daring highwaymen, who work openly.

It is thought there can be no doubt but that the Youngers were among the gang that attacked the train at Gad's Hill, in 1873, as it was one of the boldest robberies on record, the passengers in an entire train being intimidated and robbed by a few men.

Cole Younger was one of the principal actors in the Northfield tragedy, leading the squad which dashed through the streets to intimidate the inhabitants while his comrades robbed the bank. Undoubtedly he is accused of many crimes he never committed, but he has made himself a name that will long exist, as one of the most bold and reckless outlaws of modern times.

He claims that he is now for the first time in prison, and one cannot but wonder how, in this age of intelligence and civilization, so terrible a freebooter could have carried on his nefarious business for fourteen long years almost unmolested.

JAMES H. YOUNGER.

JAMES H. YOUNGER

The next brother, James H. Younger, is now about 29 years of age, and is one of the captives now in the State prison. He has suffered greatly from his wounds received at the time of his capture. He is a mild, inoffensive looking man, and would not be taken for a robber and murderer. He has always been the pet of the family, and after the fight at Madelia which closed his career as a bandit, his brothers Cole and Bob showed great anxiety about him.

Cole said he did not fear death as it would be over in five minutes, but he entreated the attending doctor to "exercise his utmost skill on Jim, who was always a good boy." Bob also asked several times for Jim, displaying much concern for his welfare.

When their young sister, Miss Ret Younger, visited them in their prison on the 3d of October, 1876, she was terribly excited in finding James in such a plight, and gave way to sobs and shrieks.

James joined Quantrell's company in 1863, but in the autumn of 1864 he was taken prisoner in the skirmish which resulted in the death of the notorious leader, and was incarcerated in the military prison at Alton, Ill., where he remained until the middle of 1866. He has been more domestic in his tastes than his brothers, although he has been in many desperate scrapes, and when the Northfield robbery was planned he was living in California as stated elsewhere.

BOB YOUNGER.

ROBERT E. YOUNGER

This is the youngest of the boys, being now nearly 23 years of age. He is quite prepossessing in appearance, and excited the sympathy of the ladies especially in his captivity. His career of crime extends over about three years, commencing when he was charged with horse stealing in connection with his brother John. Until that time he had remained quietly at home, being the only protector his mother had until her death, and his sister since. Bob was one of the men in the bank at Northfield and was to have taken the money.

CHARLES PITTS

This bandit who was killed at Madelia, is known throughout the south as Wells. He is presumed to be the man that shot the brave cashier. He is reputed to have been one of the most daring of southern horse thieves, and possessed a great knowledge of horses. His nature was brutal, and he was as bold and tenacious as a bull dog. The gang always engaged him when particularly dirty work was on hand, and when on a long tramp, as his horse education made him valuable in the care of stock. His body has been embalmed and is now in the possession of the surgeon-general of Minnesota, whose museum his skeleton will ultimately grace.

CHARLEY PITTS.

THE JAMES BROTHERS

It is supposed that the two robbers that succeeded in escaping, leaving six of the gang in Minnesota, three captives and three dead, were the notorious James boys, Frank and Jesse. These bandits claim, as do the Younger brothers, that they were forced to a course of crime by the aggressions of their enemies.

From the close of the war down to the present time these men have been outlaws, and a long list of crimes are laid at their door. Among others may be named the robbing of the bank at Russellville, Ky., in March, 1868. The attack on the bank of Gallaten, Mo., and the kilting of the cashier, J. W. Sheets, in December of the same year. Another bank robbery at Corydon, Iowa, in June, 1871. Another in Columbia, Ky., when the cashier was killed, and still another robbery of the bank of St. Genevieve, Mo., May, 1873. The attack on the railroad train at Gad's Hill in 1873, the more recent robbery, in December, 1875, of the express company's safe on a train on the Kansas Pacific Railroad at Muncie, where $30,000 was secured, and the Otterville robbery on the Missouri Pacific Railroad last July. All are laid to this wonderful gang of bandits which includes the James and Younger boys and a working gang of perhaps fifteen others.

In January, 1875, a desperate attempt was made to capture the James brothers by Pinkerton's detective police, by surrounding and firing the house in which their mother, now the wife of Dr. Samuels of Clay county, Mo., lived. It was a sad failure, one person being killed and several wounded. There are no good likenessess of these robbers extant, the only ones the police have being eight years old, and Cole Younger says they look nothing like them.

HEYWOOD'S BURIAL.

NAMES OF CONTRIBUTORS

At a meeting of the banks and bankers of St. Paul, Minn., Sept. 19th 1876, the following gentlemen, Henry P. Upham, Walter Mann, and John S. Prince were appointed a committee to issue a circular appeal to the banks and bankers in the United States and Canada, requesting voluntary contributions in aid of the family of Joseph Lee Heywood, late acting Cashier of the first national bank of Northfield, Minn., who was instantly killed by a pistol shot by one of the gang of Younger-James Bros., desperadoes. In answer to about seven thousand circulars that were sent out, the committee received Twelve Thousand Six Hundred and Two Dollars and Six Cents($12,6022.06), which, with the Five Thousand Dollars donated by the First National Bank of Northfield to Mrs. Heywood and her child, made the sum of Seventeen Thousand Six Hundred and Two Dollars and Six Cents, ($17,602.06), a handsome tribute to the brave and noble cashier, who sacrificed his life rather than betray his trust.

It is estimated that upwards of Ten Thousand Dollars has been expended by the First National Bank of Northfield, the State and County authorities, and private citizens, in capturing the robbers.

The following are the names of the contributors:

MASSACHUSETTS.

Monson National Bank	Monson	$5
Merchants National Bank	Salem	25
Geo. L. Ames	Salem	2
Franklin County National Bank	Greenfield	25
Adams National Bank	North Adams	20
First National Bank	Northampton	50
Lechmere National Bank	East Cambridge	25
Framingham National Bank	Framingham	50

Asiatic National Bank	Salem	25
Geo. E. Bullard	Boston	10
Salem Savings Bank	Salem	100
Safety Fund National Bank	Fitchburg	20
Naumkeag National Bank	Salem	100
National City Bank	Boston	100
C. C. Barry	//	10
Northboro National Bank	Northboro	10
Mercantile National Bank	Salem	25
Charles River National Bank	Cambridge	25
Bay State National Bank	Lawrence	50
Crocker National Bank	Turners Falls	20
South Danvers National Bank	Peabody	25
Worcester National Bank	Worcester	25
City National Bank	//	25
Central National Bank	//	25
Merchants National Bank	//	25
Security National Bank	//	25
Quinsigamond National Bank	//	25
Citizens National Bank	//	25
First National Bank	//	25
Worcester Co. Inst for Savings	//	25
Worcester Mechanics Savings Bank	//	25
People's Savings Bank	//	25
Worcester Five Cent Savings Bank	//	25

Worcester Safe Dep. & Trust Co	//	25
Salem National Bank	Salem	25
National Granite Bank	Quincy	10
Central National Bank	Lynn	20
Townsend National Bank	Townsend	10
Housatonic National Bank	Stockbridge	10
Leicester National Bank	Leicester	20
Conway National Bank	Conway	15

NEW YORK.

National Bank	West Troy	$10
Bank of America //	New York	50
Tanners National Bank	Catskill	10
J. G. Munro	Buffalo	10
Marine Bank	//	10
H. F. Spaulding, President Cen. Trust Co.	New York	10
Brown Bros. & Co	//	25
Importers & Traders National Bank	//	25
Farmers & Mechanics National Bank	Buffalo	10
F. R. Delano & Co	Niagara Falls	5

Ten Banks in	Syracuse	100
Lyons National Bank	Lyons	5
Manufacturers National Bank	Troy	25
First National Bank	New York	25
Fisk & Hatch	//	20
E. P. Cook	Havana	5
National Central Bank	Cherry Valley	10
National Bank of Salem	Salem	10
Merchants National Bank	New York	50
Munroe County Savings Bank	Rochester	5
Mechanics National Bank	New York	10
G. H. Smith	Haverstraw	10
City Bank	Oswego	10
Manufacturers National Bank	Williamsburg	10
Bank of North America	New York	25
Manhattan Co.	//	50
Metropolitan National Bank	//	150
W. W. Astor	//	500
Gallatin National Bank	//	100
Executive Commercial Mercantile Trust Co.	//	55
First National Bank	Red Hook	10
First National Bank	Jamestown	10
Farmers National Bank	Amsterdam	10
Chemical National Bank	New York	25
New York Savings Bank	//	100
American Ex. National Bank	//	25

J. T. Foote	//	50
First National Bank	Champlain	6
Witmer Bros.	Suspension Bridge	5
City National Bank	Jamestown	5
Manufacturers Bank	Cohoes	10
C. P. Williams	Albany	10
First National Bank	Rondont	20
Third National Bank	New York	50

MISSOURI.

Bank of Holden	Holden	$5
People's Savings Bank	Chilicothe	5
Third National Bank	St. Louis	25
Montgomery County Bank	Montgomery City	5
Boone County National Bank	Columbia	10
First National Bank	St. Joseph	5
Bank of Joplin	Joplin	5
First National Bank	Kansas City	10
Scotland County Bank	Memphis	5
Farmer and Drovers Bank	Carthage	5
Bank of Commerce	St. Louis	50

First National Bank	Paris	10
Lawrence County Bank	Pierce City	5
Franklin Avenue German Savings In	St. Louis	25
Waverly Bank	Waverly	5
Aull Savings Bank	Lexington	5

TENNESSEE.

First National Bank	Chattanooga	$10
Commercial National Bank	Knoxville	5

OHIO.

Jos. F. Larkin & Co	Cincinnati	$5
Ramsey & Teeple	Delta	1
Farmers Bank	Wapakoneta	5
Second National Bank	Toledo	25

First National Bank	Massillon	10
First National Bank	Portsmouth	5
Harrison National Bank	Cadiz	5
Commercial National Bank	Cleveland	20
Barber & Merrill	Wauseon	10
First National Bank	Troy	20
Merchants National Bank	Dayton	25
Youngstown Savings and Loan Association	Youngstown	25
Wicks Bros. & Co	//	10
Second National Bank	//	25
First National Bank	//	25
First National Bank	Springfield	15
First National Bank	East Liverpool	10
First National Bank	Ashland	5

MICHIGAN.

Second National Bank	Detroit	$100
Second National Bank	Hillsdale	5
First National Bank	Plymouth	10
First National Bank	St. Joseph	10
First National Bank	Port Huron	10

Randall & Darrah	Grand Rapids	10
National Bank of Michigan	Marshall	10
Boies, Rude & Co.	Hudson	5
First National Bank	Houghton	50
First National Batik	Dowagiac	10
Ann Arbor Savings Bank	Ann Arbor	10
Perkins, Thompson & Co	Hudson	5
First National Bank	Hancock	25
Merchants & Miners Bank	Calumet	15

INDIANA.

Richmond National Bank	Richmond	$5
Fort Wayne National Bank	Fort Wayne	10
Citizens National Bank	Jeffersonville	5
First National Bank	New Albany	25
Brazil Bank	Brazil	5
Walkers Bank	Kokomo	1
Citizens National Bank	Greensburg	5
National Branch Bank	Madison	25
First National Bank	Richmond	25
Citizens National Bank	Peru	10

| First National Bank | Tell City | 10 |

ILLINOIS.

First National Bank	Marseilles	$5
Commercial National Bank	Chicago	5
Chicago Clearings House Association	//	1,000
Union National Bank	Aurora	5
J. A. Beach	Bunker Hill	1
"A Friend"	Girard	1
Bank of Forreston	Forreston	2
Geo. Wright	Paxton	1.50
First National Bank	Peoria	10
First National Bank	Princeton	5
City National Bank	Cairo	5
Peoples Bank	Bloomington	5
Scott & Wrigley	Wyoming	5
C. G. Cloud	McLeansboro	5
Union National Bank	Streator	10
Knowlton Bros	Freeport	5
Alton National Bank	Alton	5
W. F. Thornton & Son	Shelbyville	25

Farmers National Bank	Keithsburg	10
First National Bank	Freeport	10
First National Bank	Kankakee	20
First National Bank	Ottawa	15
Citizens National Bank	//	15
First National Bank	Quincy	10
First National Bank	Arcola	2
Edgar Co. National Bank	Paris	5
Griggsville National Bank	Griggsville	10
Cass Co. Bank	Beardstown	5
First National Bank	Knoxville	10
T. W. Raymond & Co	Kinmundy	5
Ridgely National Bank	Springfield	5
First National Bank	Warsaw	10
First National Bank	Shawneetown	10
First National Bank	Rushville	10
Stetson, Littlewood & Richards	Farmington	10
First National Bank	Canton	10
First National Bank	Centralia	2.50

MAINE.

First National Bank	Brunswick	$10
West Waterville National Bank	West Waterville	5
First National Bank	Damariscotta	5
People's National Bank	Waterville	5
Banks in	Portland	150

VERMONT.

First National Bank	Fairhaven	$10
First National Bank	Orwell	10

ARKANSAS.

National Bank Western Arkansas Fort Smith $5

CALIFORNIA.

Bank of Woodland	Woodland	$5
Caisse d'Epargnes francaise	San Francisco	10
Kern Valley Bank	Bakersfield	5.45
First National Gold Bank	Oakland	10
Nevada Bank	San Francisco	100
Santa Barbara County Bank	Santa Barbara	10.80

COLORADO.

First National Bank	Denver	$10
First National Bank	Trinidad	1
Emerson & West	Greeley	5

Colorado National Bank   Denver   20

DAKOTA TERRITORY.

Mark M. ParmerYankton2

NEW HAMPSHIRE.

Claremont National Bank	Claremont	$10
Castleton National Bank	Castleton	5
National Bank of Lebanon	Lebanon	10
Littleton National Bank	Littleton	10

TEXAS.

Ragnet & Fry	Marshall	$10
J. R. Couts & Co	Weatherford	2
Merchants and Planters Bank	Sherman	10
First National Bank	Parsons	5

RHODE ISLAND.

Roger Williams National Bank	Providence	$25
Manufacturers National Bank	//	25
Washington National Bank	Westerly	50
National Phoenix Bank	//	15
National Exchange Bank	Providence	25
Centerville National Bank	Centreville	5
Warwick Institute for Savings	//	10
Merchants National Bank	Providence	5

CONNECTICUT.

First National Bank	Middletown	$20
First National Bank	Stamford	25
Phoenix National Bank	Hartford	50
Geo. A. Butler	New Haven	5
Banks of Bridgeport.	Bridgeport	90
Hartford National Bank	Hartford	50
Deep River National Bank	Deep River	10
Stamford National Bank	Stamford	10
Farmers & Mechanics Savings Bank	Middletown	15
Norwich Savings Bank	Norwich	20
Thames National Bank	//	30

PENNSYLVANIA.

First National Bank	Columbia	$5

First National Bink	Sharon	5
Pittsburgh Clearing House Association.	Pittsburgh	200
National Bank	Pottstown .	10
First National Bank	Oil City	10
National Bank, Chester Valley	Coatesvillle	25
First National Bank	Pittston	25
Watsontown Bank	Watsontown	5
Cassatt & Co	Philadelphia	20
First National Bank	Shippensburg	5
First National Bank Hanover	Hanover	5
First National Bank	Strasburg	5
St. Petersburg Savings Bank	St. Petersburg	2
Marine National Bank	Erie	25
National Bank, Fayette Co	Uniontown	5
National Bank, Chester Co	Chester	10
Marine National Bank	Pittsburg	25
Columbia National Bank	Columbia	10
Citizens National Bank	Ashland	15
Doylstown National Bank	Doylestown	10
Spring Garden Bank	Philadelphia	5
National Bank, Oxford	Oxford	10
First National Bank	Altoona	10
Commercial National Bank of Pennsylvania	Philadelphia	25
National Bank Republic	//	20
Union National Bank	//	10
National Bank of	Phoenixville	10
Farmers & Mechanics National Bank	//	5
Bank of North America	Philadelphia	250

IOWA.

First National Bank	Belle Plaine	5
Levitt, Johnson & Lursch	Waterloo	5
First National Bank	Boone	2
First National Bank	Wyoming	10
First National Bank	Decorah	5
National State Bank	Burlington	25
Conger, Pierce & Co	Dexter	2
E. Manning	Keosaugua	10
First National Bank	Chariton	5
Citizen's National Bank	Winterset	10
H. F. Greef & Bro	Beautonsport	5
Council Bluff Savings Bank	Council Bluff	5
Greene County Bank	Jefferson	2
Muscatine National Bank	Muscatine	10
State National Bank	Keokuk	10
First National Bank	Red Oak	10
Davenport National Bank	Davenport	25
Bank of Carroll	Carroll City	5

Cerro Gordo County Bank	Mason City	5
Clinton National Bank	Clinton	50
Silverman, Cook & Co	Muscatine	5
First National Bank	Grinnell	5

KANSAS.

Topeka National Bank	Topeka	$5
Abilene Bank	Abilene	1
Humboldt Bank	Humboldt	1
D. W. Powers & Co	Ellsworth	5
Emporia National Bank	Emporia	2
Turner & Otis	Independence	5

MARYLAND.

First National Bank	Baltimore	$50

National Union Bank	//	25
First National Bank	Westminster	5
National Bank of Baltimore	Baltimore	25

CANADA.

Merchants Bank, Canada	Hamilton	$6
Bank of Toronto	Toronto	21.90
Thos. Fyshe	Halifax	10.90

KENTUCKY.

| Theo. Schwartz & Co | Louisville | $5 |
| National Bank of Cynthiana | Cynthiana | 5 |

German National Bank   Covington   25

ALABAMA.

City National Bank   Selma $10

SOUTH CAROLINA.

South Carolina Loan & Trust Co   Charleston $15
National Bank   Anderson   20

MISSISSIPPI.

Vicksburgh BankVicksburg$10

NEW JERSEY.

First National BankMorristown$50

MINNESOTA.

First National Bank	St. Paul	$100
Second National Bank	//	100
Merchants National Bank		100
German American Bank	//	75
Dawson & Co	//	50
Marine Bank	//	25
Farmers & Mechanics Bank	//	25

Savings Bank	//	25
"A Friend"	//	50
Northwestern National Bank	Minneapolis	100
Merchants National Bank	//	10
First National Bank	//	25
National Exchange Bank	//	25
State National Bank	//	10
Hennepin County Savings Bank	//	10
Citizens National Bank	Faribault	50
C. H. Whipple	//	25
First National Bank	Kasson	25
First National Bank	Shakopee	25
First National Bank	Lake City	10
A Printer	Waseca	2
First National Bank for Customer	Le Hoy	10
Citizens National Bank	Mankato	50
Farmers National Bank	Owatonna	10
Bank of Washington	Worthington	5
First National Bank	Stillwater	25
Chadbourn Bros & Co	Blue Earth City	5
Farmers & Traders Bank	Hastings	25
O. Roos	Taylors Falls	5
First National Bank	Faribault	50
Lumbermens National Bank	Stillwater	25
H. D. Brown & Co	Albert Lea	15
First National Bank	Red Wing	25

Pierce, Simmons & Co	//	20
First National Bank	Austin	100
Bank of Farmington	Farmington	25
H. H. Bell	Duluth	5
City Bank	Minneapolis	25
Eddy & Erskine	Plainview	10
First National Bank	St. Peter	25
First National Bank	Hastings	25

WISCONSIN.

First National Bank	Milwaukee	$50
National Exchange Bank	//	25
Manufacturers National Bank	Racine	10
First National Bank	Whitewater	20
Wisconsin Marine & Fire Ins. Co. Bank	Milwaukee	50
First National Bink	Hudson	10
Bank of Evansville	Evansville	5
Batavian Bank	La Crosse	10
National Bank	Delavan	5
First National Bank	Munroe	10
Bowman & Humbird	Black River Falls	5

Milwaukee National Bank	Milwaukee	25
Second Ward Savings Bank	//	100
German Bank	Sheboygan	10
J. F. Cleghorn	Clinton	5
Savings Bank	Fond du Lac	5
Kellogg National Bank	Green Bay	25
First National Bank	Madison	10
Waukesha National Bank	Waukesha	10
Marshall & Ilsley	Milwaukee	25
Shullsburg Bank	Shullsburg	5
First National Bank	Fond du Lac	10
Humphry & Clark	Bloomington	5

DELAWARE.

Delaware City National Bank	Delaware	$10
First National Bank	Wilmington	25
Union National Bank	//	20
National Bank of Delaware	//	10
National Bank of Wilmington & B. W.	//	20

Newport National Bank	Newport	20

WEST VIRGINIA.

Merchants National Bank of W. Virginia	Morganstown	$5
Commercial Bank	Wheeling	10
Exchange Bank	//	5

VIRGINIA.

Planters & Mechanics Bank	Petersburg	$10
German Banking Company	.Alexandria	5

LOUISIANA.

Citizens Bank of LouisianaNew Orleans$ 10

GEORGIA.

Bank of AmericusAmericus$1

UTAH

Deseret National BankSalt Lake City$10

OREGON.

First National Bank	Portland	$50
Ladd & Tilton	//	5
"Unknown"		2

Collected by a Committee of Associated Banks in Boston, Massachusetts.
H. W. PICKERING, Chairman.

Taunton National Bank	Taunton	$30
Old Boston National Bank	Boston	100
Second // //	//	100
Merchants // //	//	150
Howard // //		100
Suffolk //	//	100
Faneuil Hall //	//	100
Blackstone // //	//	100
Tremont // //	//	100

Exchange // //	//	100
Maverick // //	//	100
Revere // //	//	100
North // //	//	100
Shoe & Leather // //	//	100
Shawmut // //	//	100
Everett // //	//	50
Third // //	//	50
Eagle // //	//	50
Traders // //	//	50
First // //	//	50
Market // //	//	50
Redemption // //	//	50
Webster National Bank	Boston	50
Hamilton // //	//	50
Freemans // //	//	50
Massachusetts // //	//	50
Boylston // //	//	50
New England // //	//	50
Hide & Leather // //	//	50
Massachusetts Hosp. Life Insurance Co	//	100

Union Sale Dep. Vaults	//	100
Appleton National Bank	Lowell	50
Railroad National Bank	//	25
Chapin Banking Company	Springfield	50
Bank of Brighton	Brighton	30
Warren National Bank	Peabody	25
Millers Rivers National Bank	Athol	25
First National Bank	Greenfield	25
Cambridge City National Bank	Cambridge	15
Pacific National Bank	Nantucket	15
Merchants National Bank	Newburyport	15
Newburyport Savings Bank	//	20
First National Bank	//	20
Ocean National Bank	//	15
Mechanics National Bank	//	15
Five Cent Savings Bank	//	10
Cambridgeport National Bank	Cambridgeport	15
National City Bank	Lynn	25
American National Bank	Hartford, Conn	25
Mercantile National Bank	//	25
Birmingham National Bank	Birmingham, Conn	20
Central National Bank	Middletown, //	15
Waterbury National Bank	Waterbury, //	200
Middlesex County National Bank	Middletown, //	10
Employees of above bank	//	10

New Haven County National Bank	New Haven, //	10
First National Bank	Augusta, Maine	25
Granite // //	// //	25
First // //	Concord, //	25
Calais // //	Calais, //	10
Freemans // //	Augusta, //	10
Kennebec Savings Bank	//	10
Cabasse National //	Gardiner //	10
Gardiner // //	//	5
Bath // //	Bath //	5
Falls Village Savings Bank	//	5
Third National //	Providence, R; I.	25
Bank of North America	// //	20
Slater National Bank	Pawtucket, //	50
Rhode Island National Bank	Weybasset, //	10
Niantic National Bank	Westerley, //	10
Rhode Island National Bank	// //	10
Rockingham National Bank	Portsmouth, N. H.	20
Strafford National Bank	Dover, N. H..	10
National State Capital Bank	Concord, N. H.	25
Bank of Derby Line	Derby, Vt	10
Montpielier National Bank	Montpelier, Vt.	20

Total amount collected by committee of associated Banks of Boston
$3430